The Torch

The Torch

EIGHT LECTURES ON RACE POWER IN LITERATURE DELIVERED BEFORE THE LOWELL INSTITUTE OF BOSTON MCMIII

GEORGE EDWARD WOODBERRY

AUGESCUNT ALIAE GENTES, ALIAE MINUUNTUR,
INQUE BREVI SPATIO MUTANTUR SAECLA ANIMANTUM
ET QUASI CURSORES VITAI LAMPADA TRADUNT

Essay Index Reprint Series

BOOKS FOR LIBRARIES PRESS
FREEPORT, NEW YORK

First Published 1905
Reprinted 1969

STANDARD BOOK NUMBER:
8369-1115-6

LIBRARY OF CONGRESS CATALOG CARD NUMBER:
73-84349

PRINTED IN THE UNITED STATES OF AMERICA

CONTENTS

The Torch

I

MAN AND THE RACE

It belongs to a highly developed race to become, in a true sense, aristocratic — a treasury of its best in practical and spiritual types, and then to disappear in the surrounding tides of men. So Athens dissolved like a pearl in the cup of the Mediterranean, and Rome in the cup of Europe, and Judæa in the cup of the Universal Communion. Though death is the law of all life, man touches this earthen fact with the wand of the spirit, and transforms it into the law of sacrifice. Man has won no victory over his environment so sublime as this, finding in his mortal sentence the true choice of the soul and in the road out of Paradise the open highway of eternal life. Races die; but the ideal of sacrifice as the highest race-destiny has seldom occurred to men, though it has been suggested both by devout Jews and by devout Irishmen as the divinely appointed organic law of the Hebrew and the Celt. In the general view of men the extinction of a race partakes of the unreasoning finality of nature.

The vital flow of life has this in common with disease — that it is self-limited; the fever runs its course, and burns away. "All thoughts, all passions, all delights," have this history. In the large arcs of social being, movements of the human spirit, however embracing and profound, obey the same law of the limitation of specific energy. Revolutions, reforms, re-births exhaust their fuel, and go out. Races are only greater units of man; for a race, as for an individual, there is a time to die; and that time, as history discloses it, is the moment of perfection. This is the largest fact in the moral order of the world; it is the centre of providence in history. In the life of the human spirit the death of the best of its achieving elements, in the moment of their consummation, is as the fading of the flower of the field or the annual fall of the leaves of the forest in the natural world; and unless this be a sacrificial death, it were wantonness and waste like the deaths of nature; but man and his works are supernatural, and raised above nature by an imperishable relation which they contain. Race-history is a perpetual celebration of the Mass. The Cross initials every page with its broad gold, and he whose eye misses that letter has lost the clue to the meaning. I do not refer to the self-devotion of individuals, the sacred lives of the race. I speak of the involuntary element in the life of nations, or what seems such on the vast scale of social life. Always some great culture is dying to enrich the soil of new harvests, some civilization is crumbling to rubbish to be the hill of a more beautiful city, some race is spending itself that a lower and barbarous world may inherit its stored treasure-house. Although no race may consciously devote itself to the higher ends of mankind, it is the prerogative of its men of genius so to devote it; nor is any nation truly great which is not so dedicated by its warriors and statesmen, its saints and heroes, its thinkers and dreamers. A nation's poets are its true owners; and by the stroke of the pen they convey the title-deeds of its real possessions to strangers and aliens.

This dedication of the energy of a race by its men of genius to the higher ends of mankind is the sap of all the world. The spiritual life of mankind spreads, the spiritual unity of mankind grows, by this age-long surrender of privilege and power into the hands of the world's new men, and the leavening of the mass by the best that has anywhere arisen in it, which is thus brought about. The absorption of aristocracies in democracies, the dissolution of the nobler product in inferior environments, the salutary death of cultures, civilizations, breeds of men, is the strict line on which history, drawing the sundered parts of the earth slowly together, moves to that great consummation when the best that has at any time been in the world shall be the portion of every man born into it. If the old English blood, which here on this soil gave birth to a nation, spread civilization through it, and cast the orbit of its starry course in time, is destined to be thus absorbed and lost in the nation which it has formed, we should be proud and happy in such a fate; for this is to wear the seal of God's election in history. Nay, if the aristocracy of the whole white race is so to melt in a world of the coloured races of the earth, I for one should only rejoice in such a divine triumph of the sacrificial idea in history; for it would mean the humanization of mankind.

Unless this principle is strongly grasped, unless there be an imperishable relation in man and his works which they contain, and which, though it has other phases, here appears in this eternal salvage stored up in a slowly perfecting race, history through its length and breadth is a spectacle to appall and terrify the reason. The perpetual flux of time —

> " *Sceptres, tiaras, swords, and chains, and tomes*
> *Of reasoned wrong, glozed on by ignorance* "—

is a mere catastrophe of blood and error unless its mighty subverting and dismaying changes are related to something which does not pass away with dethroned gods, abandoned empires and repealed codes of law and morals. But in the extinction of religions, in imperial revolutions, in the bloody conflict of ideas, there is one thing found stable; it is the mind itself, growing through ages. That which in its continuity we call the human spirit, abides. Men, tribes, states disappear, but the race-mind endures. A conception of the world and an emotional response thereto constitute the life of the race-mind, and fill its consciousness with ideas and feelings, but in these there is no element of chance, contingency or frailty; they are master-ideas, master-emotions, clothed with the power of a long reign over men, and imposing themselves upon each new generation almost with the yoke of necessity. What I designate as the race-mind — the sole thing permanent in history — is this potentiality of thought and feeling, in any age, realizing itself in states of mind and habits of action long established in the race, deeply inherited, and slowly modified. The race-mind is the epitome of the past. It contains all human energy, knowledge, experience, that survives. It is the resultant of millions of lives whose earthly power it stores in one deathless force.

This race-mind is simply formed. Life presents certain permanent aspects in the environment, which generates way of behaviour thereto, normal and general among men. The world is a multiplicity, a harvest-field, a battle-ground; and thence arises through human contact ways of numbering, or mathematics, ways of tillage, or agriculture, ways of fighting, or military tactics and strategy, and these are incorporated in individuals as habits of life. The craftsman has the mind of his craft. Life also presents certain other permanent internal aptitudes in the soul, whence arisest the mind of the artist, the inventor, the poet. But this cast of mind of the mathematician or of the painter is rather a phase of individual life. In the larger unit of the race, environment and aptitude working together in the historic life of ages develop ideas, moods and energies characteristic of the race in which they occur. In the sphere of ideas, freedom is indissolubly linked with the English, righteousness with the Hebrew; in the temperamental sphere, a signal instance is the Celtic genius — mystery, twilight, supernatural fantasy, lamentation, tragic disaster — or the Greek genius, definiteness, proportioned beauty, ordered science, philosophic principle; and, in the sphere of energy, land and gold hunger, and that strange soul-hunger — hunger to possess the souls of men — which is at the root of all propagandism, have been motive powers in many races.

Thus, in one part or another of time and place, and from causes within and without, the race, coming to its best, flowers in some creative hope, ripens in some shaping thought, glows in some resistless enthusiasm. Each of these in its own time holds an age in its grasp. They seize on men and shape them in multitudes to their will, as the wind drives the locusts; make men hideous ascetics, send them on forlorn voyages, devote them to the block and the stake, make Argonauts, Crusaders, Lollards of them, fill Europe in one age with a riot of revolution and in the next with the camps of tyrannic power. These ideas, moods, energies have mysterious potency; they seem to possess an independent being; though, like all the phenomena of life-energy they are self-limited, the period of their growth, culmination and decline extends through generations and centuries; they seem less the brood of man's mind than higher powers that feed on men. They are surrounded by a cloud of witnesses — fanatics, martyrs, dupes; they doom whole peoples to glory or shame; in the undying battle of the soul they are the choosers of the slain. Though they proceed from the human spirit, they rule it; and in life they are the spiritual presences which are most closely unveiled to the apprehension, devotion and love of men.

The race-mind building itself from immemorial time out of this mystery of thought and passion, as generation after generation kneels and fights and fades, takes unerringly the best that anywhere comes to be in the world, holds to it with the cling of fate, and lets all else fall to oblivion; out of this best it has made, and still fashions, that enduring world of idea and emotion into which we are born as truly as into the natural world. It has a marvellous economy.

> "*One accent of the Holy Ghost*
> *The heedless world has never lost.*"

Egypt, India, Greece and Rome, Italy, the English, France, America, the Turk, the Persian, the Russian, the Japanese, the Chinese, the Negro feed its pure tradition of what excellence is possible to the race-mind, and has grown habitual in its being; and, as in the old myth, it destroys its parent, abolishing all these differences of climate, epoch and skull. The race-mind unifies the race which it preserves; that is its irresistible line of advance. It wipes out the barriers of time, language and country. It undoes the mischief of Babel, and restores to mankind one tongue in which all things can be understood by all men. It fuses the Bibles of all nations in one wisdom and one practice. It knocks off the tribal fetters of caste and creed; and, substituting thought for blood as the bond of the world, it slowly liberates that free soul, which is one in all men and common to all mankind. To free the soul in the individual life, and to accomplish the unity of mankind — that is its work.

To share in this work is the peculiar and characteristic office of literature. This fusion of the nations of the earth, this substitution of the thought-tie for the blood-tie, this enfranchisement of the soul, is its chief function; for literature is the organ of the race-mind. That is why literature is immortal. Though man's inheritance is bequeathed in many ways — the size and shape of the skull, the physical predisposition of the body, oral tradition, monumental and artistic works, institutions — civilization ever depends in an increasing degree upon literature both for expression and tradition; and whatever other forms the race-mind may mould itself into, literature is its most universal and comprehensive form. That is why literature is the great conservator of society. It shares in the life of the race-mind, partakes of its nature, as language does of thought, corresponds to it accurately, duplicates it, is its other-self. It is through literature mainly that we know the race-mind, and come to possess it; for though the term may seem abstract, the thing is real. Men of genius are great in proportion as they share in it, and national literatures are great in proportion as they embody and express it. Bruntière, the present critic of France, has recently announced a new literary formula. He declares that there is a European literature, not the combined group of national literatures, but a single literature common to European civilization, and that national literatures in their periods of culmination, are great in proportion as they coincide for the time being with this common literature, feed it, and, one after another taking the lead, create it. The declaration is a gleam of self-consciousness in the unity of Europe. How slowly the parts of a nation recognize the integrity of their territory and the community of their interests is one of the constant lessons of history; the Greek confederation, the work of Alfred or of Bismarck, our own experience in the Revolutionary period illustrate it; so the unity of Europe is still half-obscure and dark, though Catholicism, the Renaissance, the Reformation, the Revolution in turn flashed this unity forth, struggling to realize itself in the common civilization. The literature of Europe is the expression of this common genius — the best that man has dreamed or thought or done, has found or been, in Europe — now more brilliant in one capital, now in another as the life ebbs from state to state, and is renewed; for, though it fail here or there, it never ceases. This is the burning of the race-mind, now bright along the Seine, the Rhine and the Thames, as once by the Ganges and the Tiber. The true unity of literature, however, does not lie in the literature of Europe or of India or of antiquity, or in any one manifestation, but in that world-literature which is the organ of the race-mind in its entire breadth and wholeness. The new French formula is a brilliant application, novel, striking and arresting, of the old and familiar idea that civilization in its evolution in history is a single process, continuous, advancing and integral, of which nations and ages are only the successive phases. The life of the spirit in mankind is one and universal, burns with the same fires, moves to the same issues, joins in a single history; it is the race-mind realizing itself cumulatively in time, and mainly through the inheriting power of great literature.

I have developed this conception of the race-mind at some length because it is a primary idea. The nature of literature, and the perspective and interaction of particular literatures, are best comprehended in its light. I emphasize it. The world-literature, national literatures, individual men of genius, are what they are by virtue of sharing in the race-mind, appropriating it and identifying themselves with it; and what is true of them, on the great scale and in a high degree, is true also of every man who is born into the world. A man is a man by participating in the race-mind. Education is merely the process by which he enters it, avails himself of it, absorbs it. In the things of material civilization this is plain. All the callings of men, arts, crafts, trades, sciences, professions, the entire round of practical life, have a body of knowledge and method of work which are like gospel and ritual to them; apprentice, journeyman and master are the stages of their career; and if anything be added, from life to life, it is on a basis of ascertained fact, of orthodox doctrine and fixed practice. I suppose technical education is most uniform, and by definiteness of aim and economy of method is most efficient; and in the professions as well as in the arts and crafts competition places so high a premium on knowledge and skill that the mastery of all the past can teach is compulsory in a high degree. Similarly, in society, the material unities such as those which commerce, manufacturing, banking establish and spread, are soonest evident and most readily accepted; so true is this that the peace of the world is rather a matter of finance than of Christianity. These practical activities and the interests that spring out of them lie in the sphere of material civilization; but the race-mind, positive, enduring and beneficent as it is in that sphere, is there parcelled out and individualized, and gives a particular and almost private character to man and classes of men, and it seeks a material good. There is another and spiritual sphere in which the soul which is one and the same in all men comes to self-knowledge, has its training, and achieves its mastery of the world. Essential, universal manhood is found only here; for it is here that the race-mind, by participation in which a man is a man, enfranchizes the soul and gives to it the citizenship of the world. Education in the things of the spirit is often vague in aim and may seem wasteful in method, and it is not supported by the thrust and impetus of physical need and worldly hope; but it exists in all men in some measure, for no one born in our civilization is left so savage, no savage born in the wild is left so primitive but that he holds a mental attitude, however obscure, toward nature, man and God, and has some discipline, however initial, in beauty, love and religion. These things lie in the sphere of the soul. It is, nevertheless, true that the greatest inequalities of condition exist here, and not in that part of life where good is measured by the things of fortune. The difference between the outcast and the millionaire is as nothing to that between the saint and the criminal, the fool and the knower, the boor and the poet. It is a blessing in our civilization, and one worthy of the hand of Providence, that if in material things justice be a laggard and disparities of condition be hard to remedy, the roads to church and school are public highways, free to all. This charter of free education in the life of the soul, which is the supreme opportunity of an American life, is an open door to the treasury of man's spirit. There whosoever will shall open the book of all the world, and read and ponder, and shall enter the common mind of man which is there contained and avail of its wisdom and absorb its energies into his own and become one with it in insight, power and hope, and ere he is aware shall find himself mingling with the wisest, the holiest, the loveliest, as their comrade and peer. He shall have poet and sage to sup with him, and their meal shall be the bread of life.

What, then, is the position of the youth — of any man whose infinite life lies before him — at his entrance on this education, on this attempt to become one with the mind of the race ? and, to neglect the material side of life, what is the process by which he begins to live in the spirit, and not as one new-born, but even in his youth sharing in the wisdom and disciplined power of a soul that has lived through all human ages — the soul of mankind ? We forget the beginnings of life; we forget first sensation, first action, and the unknown magic by which, as the nautilus builds its shell, we built out of these early elements this world of the impalpable blue walls, the ocean and prairie floors, and star-sown space, each one of us for ourselves. There is a thought, which I suppose is a commonplace and may be half-trivial, but it is one that took hold of me in boyhood with great tenacity, and stirred the sense of strangeness and marvel in life; the idea that all I knew or should ever know was through something that had touched my body. The ether-wave envelopes us as the ocean, and in that small surface of contact is the sphere of sensibility — of light, sound, and the rest — out of which arises the world which each one of us perceives. It seems a fantastic conception, but it is a true one. For me the idea seemed to shrink the world to the dark envelope of my own body. It served, however, to initiate me in the broader conception that the soul is the centre, and that life — the world — radiates from it into the enclosing infinite. Wordsworth, you remember, in his famous image of our infancy presents the matter differently; for him the infant began with the infinite, and boy and man lived in an ever narrowing world, a contracting prison, like that fabled one of the Inquisition, and in the end life became a thing common and finite:

> "*Heaven lies about us in our infancy!*
> *Shades of the prison-house begin to close*
> *Upon the growing boy,*
> *But he beholds the light, and whence it flows,*
> *He sees it in his joy:*
>
> . . . .
>
> *At length the man perceives it die away,*
> *And fade into the light of common day.*"

This was never my own conception, nor do I think it is natural to many men. On the contrary, life is an expansion. The sense of the larger world comes first, perhaps, in those unremembered years when the sky ceases to be an inverted bowl, and lifts off from the earth. The experience is fixed for me by another half-childish memory, the familiar verses of Tom Hood in which he describes his early home. You will recall the almost nursery rhymes:

> "*I remember, I remember*
> *The fir-trees dark and high;*
> *I used to think their slender tops*
> *Were close against the sky;*
> *It was a childish ignorance,*
> *But now 't is little joy*
> *To know I 'm farther off from Heaven*
> *Than when I was a boy.*"

Sentiment in the place of philosophy, the thought is the same as Wordsworth's, but the image is natural and true. The noblest image, however, that sets forth the spread of the world, is in that famous sonnet by an obscure poet, Blanco White, describing the first time that the sun went down in Paradise:

> "*Mysterious night! when our first parent knew*
> *Thee from report divine, and heard thy name,*
> *Did he not tremble for this lovely frame,*
> *This glorious canopy of light and blue?*
> *Yet, 'neath the curtain of translucent dew,*
> *Bathed in the rays of the great setting flame,*
> *Hesperus with the host of heaven came,*
> *And lo! creation widened in man's view.*"

The theory of Copernicus and the voyage of Columbus are the great historical moments of such change in the thoughts of men. As travel thus discloses the amplitude of the planet and science fills the infinite of space for the learning mind, history in its turn peoples the "dark background and abysm of time." But more marvellous than the unveiling of time and space, is that last revelation which unlocks the inward world of idea and emotion, and gives solidity to life as by a third dimension. It is this world which is the realm of imaginative literature; scarcely by any other interpreter shall a man come into knowledge of it with any adequacy; and here the subject draws to a head, for it is by the operation of literature in this regard that the race-mind takes possession of the world.

We are plunged at birth *in medias res*, as the phrase is, into the midst of things — into a world already old, of old ideas, old feelings, old experience, that has drunk to the lees the wisdom of the preacher of Ecclesiastes, and renews in millions of lives the life that has been lived a million times; a world of custom and usage, of immemorial habits, of causes prejudged, of insoluble problems, of philosophies and orthodoxes and things established; and yet, too, a world of the undiscovered. The youth awakes in this world, intellectually, in literature; and since the literature of the last age is that on which the new generation is formed, he now first comes in contact with the large life of mankind in the literature of the last century. It is an extraordinary miscellaneous literature, varied and copious in matter, full of conflicting ideas, cardinal truths, and hazardous guesses; and for the young mind the problem of orientation — that is of finding itself, of knowing the true East, is difficult. Literature, too, has an electric stimulation, and in the first onrush of the intellectual life brings that well-known storm and stress which is the true awakening; with eager and delighted surprise the soul feels fresh sensibilities and unsuspected energies rise in its being. It is a time of shocks, discoveries, experiences that change the face of the world. Reading the poets, the youth finds new dynamos in himself. A new truth unseals a new faculty in him; a new writer unlooses a new force in him; he becomes, like Briareus, hundred-handed, like Shakspere, myriad-minded. So like a miracle is the discovery of the power of life.

Let me illustrate the experience in the given case — the literature of the nineteenth century. It will all fall under three heads: the world of nature's frame, the world of man's action, the world of God's being. Nature is, in the first instance, a spectacle. One may see the common sights of earth, and still have seen little. The young eye requires to be trained in what to see, what to choose to see out of the vague whole, and so to see his true self reflected there in another form, for in the same landscape the farmer, the military engineer, the painter see each a different picture. Burns teaches the young heart to see nature realistically, definitely, in hard outline, and always in association with human life — and the presence of animals friendly and serviceable to man, the life of the farm, is a dominant note in the scene. Byron guides the eye to elemental grandeur in the storm and in the massiveness of Alp and ocean. Shelley brings out colour and atmosphere and evokes the luminous spirit from every star and dew-drop and dying wave. Tennyson makes nature an artist's easel where from poem to poem glows the frescoing of the walls of life. Thus changing from page to page the youth sees nature with Burns as a man who sympathizes with human toil, with Byron as a man who would mate with the tempest, with Shelley as a man of almost spiritualized senses, with Tennyson as a man of artistic luxury. Again, nature is an order, a law in matter, such as science conceives her; and this phase appears inceptively in "Queen Mab" and explicitly in "In Memoriam," and many a minor poem of Tennyson, not the less great because minor in his work, in which alone the scientific spirit of the age has found utterance equal to its own sublimity. Yet, again, nature is a symbol, an expression of truth itself in another medium than thought; and so, in minute ways, Burns moralized the "Mountain Daisy," and Wordsworth the

"Small Celadine;" and, on the grand scale, Shelley mythologized nature in vast oracular figures of man's faith, hope, and destiny. And again, nature is a moulding influence so close to human life as to be a spiritual presence about and within it. This last feeling of the participation of nature in life is so fundamental that no master of song is without it; but, in this group, Wordsworth is pre-eminent as its exponent, with such directness, certainty and power did he seize and express it. What he saw in his dalesmen was what the mountains had made them; what he told in "Tintern Abbey" was nature making of him; what he sang in his lyric of ideal womanhood was such an intimacy of nature with woman's being that it was scarcely to be divided from her spirit. The power which fashions us from birth, sustains the vital force of the body, and feeds its growing functions, seems to exceed the blind and mute region of matter, and feeding the senses with colour, music and delight shapes the soul itself and guides it, and supports and consoles the child it has created in mortality. I do not overstate Wordsworth's sense of this truth; and it is a truth that twines about the roots of all poetry like a river of life. It explains to the growing boy something in his own history, and he goes on in the paths he has begun to follow, it may be with touches of vague mystery but with an expectant, receptive and responsive heart. In regard to nature, then, the youth's life under the favour of these poets appreciates her in at least these four ways, artistically, scientifically, symbolically and spiritually, and begins to fix in moulds of his own spirit that miracle of change, the Protean being of matter.

To turn to the world of man's life, the simplest gain from contact with this literature of which I am speaking is in the education of the historic sense. Romance discovered history, and seeking adventure and thriving in what it sought, made that great find, the Middle Ages, which the previous time looked on much as we regard the civilization of China with mingled ignorance and contempt. It found also the Gæl and the Northmen, and many an outlying region, many a buried tract of time. In Scott's novels characteristically, but also in countless others, in the rescued and revived ballad of England and the North, and in the renewed forms of Greek imagination, the historic sense is strongly drawn on, and no reader can escape its culture, for the place of history and its inspirational power in literature is fundamental in the spirit of the nineteenth century. But what most arrests the young heart, in this world of man's life, is those ideas which we sum up as the Revolution, and the principle of democracy which is primary in the literature of the last age. There the three great words — liberty, fraternity and equality — and the theory that in Shelley was so burning an enthusiasm and in Byron so passionate a force, are still aflame; and the new feeling toward man which was implicit in democracy is deeply planted in that aspect of fraternity which appears in the interest in the common lot, and in that aspect of liberty which appears in the sense of the dignity of the individual. Burns, Scott, Dickens illustrate the one; Byron, Shelley and Carlyle the other. The literature of the great watchwords, the literature of the life of the humble classes, the literature of the rebellious individual will — the latter flashing out many a wild career and exploding many a startling theory of how life is to be lived — are the very core and substance of the time. The application of ideas to life in the large, of which Rousseau was so cardinal an example, opens an endless field in a century so rich in discovery, so active in intellect and so plastic in morals; and here one may wander at will. Here is matter for a lifetime. But without particularizing, it is plain how variously, how profoundly and vividly through this literature the mind is exercised in the human world, takes on the colour, picturesqueness and movement of history, builds up the democratic social faith and develops the energy of individual freedom, and becomes a place for the career of great ideas.

There remains the world of God's being, or to vary the phrase in sympathy with the mode of approach characteristic of the nineteenth century, the world in which God is. It may be broadly stated that the notion of what used to be called an absentee God, a far-off Ruler overseeing by modes analogous to human administration the affairs of earth as a distant province, finds no place in this literature of the last age. The note of thought is rather of the intimacy of God with his creation and with the soul of man. God is known in two ways; as an idea in the intellect and as an experience in the emotions; and in poetry the two modes blend, and often blur where they blend. Their habitual expression in the great poets of the age is in pantheistic forms, but this is rather a matter of form than of substance. The immanence of the divine is the root-idea; in Wordsworth it is an immanence of sublime power, seized through communion with nature; in Shelley, who was more profoundly human, it is an immanence of transcendent love, seized through his sense of the destiny of the universe that carries in its bosom the glory of life; in Tennyson, in whom the sense of a veiled intellect was more deep, it is an immanence of mystery in both the outer and the inner world. In other parts of the field, God is also conceived in history, and there immanent as Providence. His immanence in the individual — a matter dark to any thought — is most explicitly set forth by Emerson. It is perhaps generally considered that in the literature of the ninteenth century there is a large sceptical and atheistic element; but this is an error. Genius by its own nature has no part in the spirit that denies; it is positive, affirms and creates. Its apparent denials will be found to be partial, and affect fragments of a dead past only; its denials are, in reality, higher and more universal affirmations. If Wordsworth appears to put nature in the place of God, or Shelley love, or Keats beauty, they only affirm that phase of the divine which is nighest to their own apprehension, affection and delight. Their experience of the divine governs and blends with their intellectual theory, sometimes, as I have said, with a blur of thought. Each one's experience in these things is for himself alone, and private; the ways of the Spirit no man knows; but it is manifest that for the opening mind, whether of youth or of older years, the sense of eternity, however delicate, subtle and silent is its realm, is fed nobly, sweetly and happily, by these poets in whom the spirit of man crying for expression unlocks the secrecy of its relations to the infinite.

Such is the nature of the contact of the mind with literature by means of which it enters on its race inheritance of idea and emotion, takes possession of the stored results, clothes itself with energies whose springs are in the earliest distance of time, and builds up anew for itself the whole and various world as it has come to be known by man in his age-long experience. The illustration I have employed minimizes the constancy, the completeness, the vastness of the process; for it takes no account of other disciplines, of religious tradition and practice, of oral transmission, and of such universal and intimate formative powers as mere language. But it will be found on analysis that all of these depend, in the main, on literature in the broad sense; and, in the education of the soul in the higher life, the awakening, the revealing and upbuilding force lies, I am persuaded, in the peculiar charge of literature in which the race-mind has stamped an image of itself.

It is obvious that what I have advanced, brings the principle of authority into a cardinal place in life, and clothes tradition with great power. It might seem that the individual in becoming one with the race-mind has only to endue himself with the past as with a garment, to take its mould with the patience of clay, and to be in the issue a recast of the past, thinking old thoughts, feeling old emotions, doing old actions, in pre-established ways. But this is to misconceive the process by which the individual effects this union; he does not take the impress of the race-mind as the wax receives the imprint of the seal. This union is an act of life, a process of energy, joy and growth, of self-expression; here learning is living, and there is no other way to know the doctrine than to do its will; so the race-mind is not copied, but is perpetually re-born in men, and the world which each one of us thus builds for himself out of his preferred capacities, memories and desires — our farmer's, engineer's, painter's world, as I have said — is his own original and unique world. There is none like it, none. Originality consists in this re-birth of the world in the young soul. This world, nevertheless, the world of each of us, is not one of wilfulness, fantasy and caprice; if, on the one hand, it is such stuff as dreams are made of, on the other it is the stuff of necessity. It has a consistency, a law and fate, of its own, which supports, wields and sustains it. Authority is no more than the recognition of and obedience to this underlying principle of being, whose will is disclosed to us in man's life so far as that life in its wholeness falls within our view; in knowledge of this will all wisdom consists, of its action in us all experience is woven, and in union with it all private judgment is confirmed. Authority, truly interpreted, is only another phase of that identity of the soul in all men by virtue of which society exists, and especially that intellectual state arises, that state which used to be called the republic of letters and which is the institution of the race-mind to be the centre, the home and hope of civilization in all ages — that state where the unity of mankind is accomplished in the spiritual unities of science, art and love.

To sum up these suggestions which I have thought it desirable to offer in order that the point of view taken in these lectures might, perhaps, be plain, I conceive of history as a single process in which through century after century in race after race the soul of man proceeds in a progressive comprehension of the universe and evolution of its own humanity, and passes on to each new generation its accumulated knowledge and developed energies, in their totality and without loss, at the acme of achievement. I conceive of this inheriting and bequeathing power as having its life and action in the race-mind. I conceive of literature as an organ of the race-mind, and of education as the process by which the individual enters into the race-mind, becomes more and more man, and in the spiritual life mainly by means of literature. I conceive of the body of men who thus live and work in the soul as constituting the intellectual state, that republic of letters, in which the race-mind reaches, from age to age, its maximum of knowledge and power, in men of genius and those whose lives they illumine, move and direct; the unity of mankind is the ideal end of this state, and the freeing of the soul which takes place in it is its means. I conceive of the progressive life of this state, in civilization after civilization, as a perpetual death of the best, in culture after culture, for the good of the lower, a continuing sacrifice, in the history of humanity, of man for mankind. And from this mystery, though to some it may seem only the recourse of intellectual despair, I pluck a confident faith in that imperishable relation which man and his works contain, and which though known only in the continuity of the race-mind, I am compelled to believe, has eternal reality.

The Torch

II

THE LANGUAGE OF ALL THE WORLD

The language of literature is the language of all the world. It is necessary to divest ourselves at once of the notion of diversified vocal and grammatical speech which constitutes the various tongues of the earth, and conceals the identity of image and logic in the minds of all men. Words are intermediary between thought and things. We express ourselves really not through words, which are only signs, but through what they signify — through things. Literature is the expression of life. The question, then, is — what things has literature found most effectual to express life, and has therefore habitually preferred? and what tradition in consequence of this habit of preference has been built up in all literatures, and obtained currency and authority in this province of the wider realm of all art? It is an interesting question, and fundamental for any one who desires to appreciate literature understandingly.

Perhaps you will permit me to approach it somewhat indirectly.

You are all familiar with something that is called poetic diction — that is, a selected language specially fitted for the uses of poetry; and you are, perhaps, not quite so familiar with the analogous feature in prose, which is now usually termed preciosity, or preciousness of language, that is, a highly refined and aesthetic diction, such as Walter Pater employs. The two are constant products of language that receives any literary cultivation, and they are sometimes called diseases of language. Thus, in both early and late Greek there sprang up literary styles of expression, involving the preference of certain words, constructions and even cadences, and the teaching of art in these matters was the business of the Greek rhetorician; so in Italy, Spain, and France, in the Renaissance, similar styles, each departing from the common and habitual speech of the time, grew up, and in England you identify this mood of language in Elizabeth's day as Euphuism. The phenomenon is common, and belongs to the nature of language. Poetic diction, however, you perhaps associate most clearly with the mannerism in language of the eighteenth century in England, when common and so-called vulgar words were exiled from poetry, and Gray, for example, could not speak of the Eton schoolboys as playing hoop, but only as "chasing the rolling circles' speed," and when, to use the stock example, all green things were "verdant." This is fixed in our memory because Wordsworth has the credit of leading an attack on the poetic diction of that period, both critically in his prefaces and practically in his verse; he went to the other extreme, and introduced into his poetry such homely words as "tub," for example; he held that the proper language of poetry is the language of common life. So Emerson in his addresses, you remember, had recourse to the humblest objects for illustration, and shocked the formalism of his time by speaking of "the meal in the firkin, the milk in the pan." He was applying in prose the rule of Wordsworth in poetry. Walt Whitman represents the extreme of this use of the actual language of men. But if you consider the matter, you will see that this choice of the homely word only sets up at last a fashion of homeliness in the place of a fashion of refinement, and breeds, for instance, dialect poets in shoals; and often the choice is really not of the word, but of the homely thing itself as the object of thought and expressive image of it; and in men so great as Emerson and Wordsworth the practice is a proof of that sympathy with common life which made them both great democrats. But in addition to the diction that characterizes an age, you must have observed that in every original writer there grows up a particular vocabulary, structure and rhythm that he affects and that in the end become his mannerism, or distinctive style, so marked that you recognize his work by its stamp alone, as in Keats, Browning, and Swinburne in poetry, and in Arnold in prose. In other words there is at work in the language of a man, or of an age even, a constant principle of selection which tends to prefer certain ways and forms of speech to others, and in the end developes a language characteristic of the age, or of the man.

This principle of selection, whether it works toward refinement or homeliness, operates in the same way. It must be remembered — and it is too often forgotten — that the problem of any artistic work is a problem of economy. How to get into the two hours' traffic of the stage the significance of a whole life, of a group of lives; how to pack into a sixteen-line lyric a dramatic situation and there sphere it in its own emotion; how to rouse passion and pour it in a three-minute poem, like Shelley's "Indian Air" — all these are problems in economy, by which speed, condensation, intensity are gained. Now words in themselves are colourless, except so far as their musical quality is concerned; but the thing that a word stands for has a meaning of its own and usually a meaning charged with associations, and often this associative meaning is the primary and important one in its use. A rose, for example, is but the most beautiful of flowers in itself, but it is so charged with association in men's lives, and still more heavily charged with long use of emotion in literature, that the very word and mere name of it awakes the heart and sets a thousand memories unconsciously vibrating. This added meaning is what I am accustomed to term an overtone in words; and it is manifest that, in view of the necessity for economy in poetic art, those words which are the richest and deepest in overtone will be preferred, because of the speed, certainty and fullness they contain. The question will be what overtones in life appeal most to this or that poet; he will reproduce them in his verse; Pope will use the overtones of a polished society, Wordsworth and Emerson those of humble life. Now our larger question is what overtones are characteristically preferred in great literature, in what objects do they most inhere, and in what way is the authoritative tradition of literature, as respects its means of expression, thus built up?

It goes without saying that all overtones are either of thought or feeling. What modes of expression, then, what material objects, what forms of imagination, what abstract principles of thought, are most deeply charged with ideas and emotions? It will be agreed that, as a mere medium, music expresses pure emotion most directly and richly; music seems to enter the physical frame of the body itself, and move there with the warmth and instancy of blood. The sound of words, therefore, cannot be neglected, and in the melody and echo of poetry sound is a cardinal element; yet, it is here only the veining of the marble, it is not the material itself. In the objects which words summon up, there is sometimes an emotional power as direct and immediate as that of music itself, as for example, in the great features of nature, the mountains, the plains, the ocean, which awe even the savage mind. But, in general, the emotional power of material objects is lent to them by association, that is by the human use that has been made of them, as on the plain of Marathon, to use Dr. Johnson's old illustration, it is the thought of what happened there that makes the spectator's patriotism "gain force" as he surveys the scene. This human use of the world is the fountain of significance in all imaginative and poetic speech; and in the broad sense history is the story of this human use of the world.

History is so much of past experience as abides in race-memory; and underlies race-literature in the same way that a poet's own experience underlies his expression of life. I do not mean that when a poet unlocks his heart, as Shakspere did in his sonnets, he necessarily writes his own biography; in the poems he writes there may be much of actual event as in Burns's love-songs, or little as in Dante's "New Life." Much of a poet's experience takes place in imagination only; the life he tells is oftenest the life that he strongly desires to live, and the power, the purity and height of his utterance may not seldom be the greater because experience here uses the voices of desire. "All I could never be," in Browning's plangent line, has been the mounting strain of the sublimest and the tenderest songs of men. All Ireland could never be, thrills and sorrows on her harp's most resonant string, and is the master-note to which her sweetest music ever returns. All man could never be makes the sad majesty of Virgil's verse. As with a man, what a nation strongly desires is no small part of its life, and is the mark of destiny upon it, whether for failure or success; so the note of world-empire is heard in the latest English verse, and the note of humanity — the service of all men — has always been dominant in our own. History, then, must be thought of, in its relation to literature, as including the desire as well as the performance of the race.

History, however, in the narrowest sense, lies close to the roots of imaginative literature. The great place of history and its inspirational power in the literature of the last century I have already referred to; it is one of the most important elements in the extraordinary reach and range of that splendid outburst of imagination throughout Europe. Aristotle recognized the value of history as an aid to the imagination, at the very moment that he elevated poetry above history. In that necessary economy of art, of which I spoke, it is a great gain to have well-known characters and familiar events, such as Agamemnon and the "Trojan War," in which much is already done for the spectator before the play begins. So our present historical novelists have their stories half-written for them in the minds of their readers, and especially avail themselves of an emotional element there, a patriotism, which they do not have to create. The use of history to the imagination, however, goes farther than merely to spare it the pains of creating character and incident and evoking emotion. It assists a literary movement to begin with race-power much as a poet's or — as in Dickens's case — a novelist's own experience aids him to develop his work, however much that experience may be finally transformed in the work. Thus the novel of the last age really started its great career from Scott's historic sense working out into imaginative expression, and in a lesser degree from so minor a writer as Miss Edgeworth in whose Irish stories — which were contemporary history — Scott courteously professed to find his own starting point. It is worth noting, also, that the Elizabethan drama had the same course. Shakspere following Marlowe's example developed from the historical English plays, in which he worked in Scott's manner, into his full control of imagination in the purely ideal sphere. History has thus often been the handmaid of imagination, and the foster-mother of great literary ages. Yet to vary Aristotle's phrase — poetry is all history could never be.

It appears to me, nevertheless, that history underlies race-literature in a far more profound and universal way. History is mortal: it dies. Yet it does not altogether die. Elements, features, fragments of it survive, and enter into the eternal memory of the race, and are there transformed, and — as we say — spiritualized. Literature is the abiding-place of this transforming power, and most profits by it. And to come to the heart of the matter, there have been at least three such cardinal transformations in the past.

The first transformation of history is mythology. I do not mean to enter on the vexed question of the origin of mythologies; and, of course, in referring to history as its ground, I include much more than that hero-worship such as you will find elaborated or invented in Carlyle's essay on Odin, and especially I include all that experience of nature and her association with human toil and moods that you will find delineated with such marvellous subtleness and fullness in Walter Pater's essay on Dionysus. In mythology, mankind preserved from his primitive experience of nature, and his own heroic past therein, all that had any lasting significance; and, although all mythologies have specific features and a particular value of their own, yet the race, coming to its best, as I have said, bore here its perfect blossom in Greek mythology. I know not by what grace of heaven, by what felicity of blend in climate, blood and the fortune of mortal life, but so it was that the human soul put forth the bud of beauty in the Greek race; and there, at the dawn of our own intellectual civilization and in the first sunrise of our poetry in Homer, was found a world filled with divine — with majestic and lovely figures, which had absorbed into their celestial being and forms the power of nature, the splendour and charm of the material sphere, the fructifying and beneficient operations of the external universe, the providence of the state and the inspiration of all arts and crafts, of games and wars and song; each of these deities was a flashing centre of human energy, aspiration, reliance — with a realm and servants of its own; and mingling with them in fair companionship was a company of demi-gods and heroes, of kings and princes, and of golden youths, significant of the fate of all young life — Adonis, Hippolytus, Orestes. This mythologic world was near to earth, and it mixed with legendary history, such history as the "Iliad" contained, and also with the private and public life of the citizens, being the ceremonial religion of the state. It was all, nevertheless, the transformation that man had accomplished of his own past, his joys and sorrows, his labours, his insights and desires, the deeds of his ancestors, — the human use that he had made of the world. This was the body of idea and emotion to which the poet appealed in that age, precisely as our historical novelists now appeal to our own knowledge of history and pre-establshed emotion with regard to it, our patriotism. Here they found a language already full charged with emotion and intelligence, of which they could avail themselves, and speaking which they spoke with the voices of a thousand years. Nevertheless, it was at best a language like others, and subject to change and decay in expressive power. The time came when, the creative impulse in mythology having ceased and its forms being fixed, the mythic world lay behind the mind of the advancing race which had now attained conceptions of the physical universe, and especially ideas of the moral life, which were no longer capable of being held in and expressed by the the mythic world, but exceeded the bounds of earlier thought and feeling and broke the ancient moulds. Then it was that Plato desired to exile the poets and their mythology from the state. He could not be content, either, with a certain change that had occurred; for the creative power in mythology having long ceased, as I have said, the imagination put forth a new function — a meditative power — and brooding over the old fables of the world of the gods discovered in them, not a record of fact, but an allegorical meaning, a higher truth which the fable contained. Mythology passed thus into an emblematic stage, in which it was again long used by mankind, as a language of universal power. Plato, however, could not free himself from the mythologic habit of imagination so planted in his race, and found the most effective expression for his ideas in the myths of his own invention which he made up by a dexterous and poetic adaptation of the old elements; and others later than Plato have found it hard to disuse the mythologic language; for, although the old religion as a thing of faith and practice died away, it survived as a thing of form and feature in art, as a phase of natural symbolism and of inward loveliness of action and passion in poetry, as a chapter of romance in the history of the race; and the modern literatures of Europe are, in large measure, unintelligible without this key.

The second great transformation of history is chivalry. Here the phenomenon is nearer in time and lies more within the field of observation and knowledge; it is possible to trace the stages of the growth of the story of Roland with some detail and precision; but, on the other hand, the Arthur myth reaches far back into the beginnings of Celtic imagination, and all such race-myths tend to appropriate and embody in themselves the characteristic features both of one another and of whatever is held to be precious and significant in history or even in classical and Eastern legend. The true growth, however, is that feudal culture, which we know as knighthood, working out its own ideal of action and character and sentiment on a basis of bravery, courtesy, and piety, and thereby generating patterns of knighthood, typical careers, and in the end an imaginative interpretation of the purest spiritual life itself in the various legends of the Holy Grail. As in the pagan world the forms and fables of mythology and their interaction downward with the human world furnished the imaginative interpretation of life as it then was, so for the mediæval age, the figures and tales of chivalry and their interaction upward with the spiritual world of Christianity, and also with the magic of diabolism round about, furnished the imaginative interpretation of that later life It was this new body of ideas and emotion in the minds of men that the mediæval poets appealed to, availed themselves of, and so spoke a language of imagery and passion that was a world-language, charged as I have said with the thought and feeling, the tradition, of a long age. What happened to the language of mythology, happened also to this language; it lost the power of reality, and men arose who, being in advance of its conceptions of life, desired to exile it, denounce it or laugh it out of existence, like Ascham in England, and Cervantes in Spain. It also suffered that late change into an allegorical or emblematic meaning, and had a second life in that form as in the notable instance of Spenser's "Færie Queene." It also could not die, but — just as mythology revived in the Alexandrian poets for a season, and fed Theocritus and Virgil — chivalry was re-born in the last century, and in Tennyson's Arthur, and in Wagner's "Parsifal" lived again in two great expressions of ideal life.

The third great transformation of history is contained in the Scriptures. The Bible is, in itself, a singularly complete expression of the whole life of a race in one volume — its faith and history blending in one body of poetry, thought and imaginative chronicle. It contains a celestial world in association with human events; its patriarchs are like demi-gods, and it has heroes, legends, tales in good numbers, and much romantic and passionate life, on the human side, besides its great stores of spirituality. In literary power it achieves the highest in the kinds of composition that it uses. It is as a whole, regarded purely from the human point of view, not unfairly to be compared in mass, variety, and scope of expression, with mythology and chivalry as constituting a third great form of imaginative language; nor has its history been dissimilar in the Christian world to which it came with something of that same remoteness in time and reality that belonged equally to mythology and chivalry. It was first used in a positive manner, as a thing of fact and solid belief; but there soon grew up, you remember, in the Christian world that habit of finding a hidden meaning in its historical record, of turning it to a parable, of extracting from it an allegorical signification. It became, not only in parts but as a whole, emblematic, and its interpretation as such was the labour of centuries. This is commonly stated as the source of that universal mood of allegorizing which characterized the mediæval world, and was as strongly felt in secular as in religious writers. Its historical tales, its theories of the universe, its cruder morals in the Jewish ages, have been scoffed at, just as was the case with the Greek myth, from the Apostate to Voltaire and later; but how great are its powers as a language is seen in the completeness with which it tyrannized over the Puritan life in England and made its history, its ideas, its emotions the habitual and almost exclusive speech of that strong Cromwellian age. In our country here in New England it gave the mould of imagination to our ancestors for two whole centuries. A book, which contains such power that it can make itself the language of life through so many centuries and in such various peoples is to be reckoned as one of the greatest instruments of race-expression that man possesses.

Mythology, chivalry, the Scriptures are the tongues of the imagination. It is far more important to know them than to learn French or German or Italian, or Latin or Greek; they are three branches of that universal language which though vainly sought on the lips of men is found in their minds and hearts. To omit these in education is to defraud youth of its inheritance; it is like destroying a long-developed organ of the body, like putting out the eye or silencing the nerves of hearing. Nor is it enough to look them up in encyclopædias and notes, and so obtain a piecemeal information; one must grow familiar with these forms of beauty, forms of honour, forms of righteousness, have something of the same sense of their reality as that felt by Homer and Virgil, by the singer of "Roland" and the chronicler of the "Mort d' Arthur," by St. Augustine, and St. Thomas. He must form his imagination upon these idealities, and load his heart with them; else many a masterpiece of the human spirit will be lost to him, and most of the rest will be impaired. If one must know vocabulary and grammar before he can understand the speech of the mouth, much more must he know well mythology, chivalry and Bible-lore before he can take possession of the wisdom that the race-mind has spoken, the beauty it has moulded life into, as a thing of passion and action, the economy of lucid power it has achieved for perfect human utterance, in these three fundamental forms of a true world-language. The literature of the last century is permeated with mythology, chivalry and to a less degree with Scripture, and no one can hope to assimilate it, to receive its message, unless his mind is drenched with these same things; and the further back his tastes and desires lead him into the literature of earlier times, the greater will be his need of this education in the material, the modes and the forms of past imagination.

It may be that a fourth great tongue of the imagination is now being shaped upon the living lips of men in the present and succeeding ages. If it be so, this will be the work of the democratic idea, which is now still at the beginning of its career; but since mythology and chivalry had their development in living men, it is natural to suppose that the human force is still operative in our own generation as it once was in those of Hellenic and mediæval years. The characteristic literature of democracy is that of its ideas, spiritualized in Shelley, and that of the common lot as represented in the sphere of the novel, spiritualized most notably in Victor Hugo. In our own country it is singular to observe that the democratic idea, though efficient in politics, does not yet establish itself in imaginative literature with any great power of brilliancy, does not create great democratic types, or in any way express itself adequately. This democratic idea, in Dickens for example, uses the experience of daily life, that is, contemporary history, or at least it uses an artistic arrangement of such experience; but the novel as a whole has given us in regard to the common lot, rather a description of life in its variety than that concentrated and essential significance of life which we call typical. If democracy in its future course should evolve such a typical and spiritualized embodiment of itself as chivalry found in Arthur and the Round Table, or as the heroic age of Greece found in Achilles and the Trojan War, or as the genius of Rome found in Aeneas and his fortunes, then imagination — race-imagination will be enriched by this fourth great instrument; but this is to cast the horoscope of too distant an hour. I introduce the thought only for the sake of including in this broad survey of race-imagination that experience of the present day, that history in the contemporary process of being transformed, out of which the mass of the books of the day are now made.

Let me recur now to that principle of selection which through the cumulative action of repeated preferences of phrase and image fixes a habit of choice which at last stamps the diction of a man, a school or an age. It is plain that in what I have called the transformation of history, of which literature is the express image, there is the same principle of selection which, working through long periods of race-life, results at last in those idealities of persons and events in which inhere most powerfully those overtones of beauty, honour and righteousness that the race has found most precious both for idea and emotion; and to these are to be added what I have had no time to include and discuss, the idealities of persons and events found outside mythology, chivalry and Scripture, in the work of individual genius like Shakspere, which nevertheless have the same ground in history, in experience, that in them is similarly transformed. Life-experience spiritualized is the formula of all great literature; it may range from the experience of a single life, like Sidney's in his sonnets to that of an empire in Virgil's "Aeneid," or of a religion in Dante's "Comedy." In either case the formula which makes it literature is the same. I have illustrated the point by the obvious spiritualizations of history. Race-life, from the point of view of literature, results at last in these moulds of imagination, and all else though slowly, yet surely, drops away into oblivion. In truth, it is only by being thus spiritualized that anything human survives from the past. The rose, I said, has been so dipped in human experience that it is less a thing of nature than a thing of passion. In the same way Adonis, Jason and Achilles, Roland and Arthur, Lancelot, Percival and Galahad, Romeo and Hamlet have drawn into themselves such myriads of human lives by admiration and love that from them everything material, contemporary and mortal has been refined away, and they seem to all of us like figures moving in an immortal air. They have achieved the eternal world. To do this is the work of art. It may seem a fantastic idea, but I will venture the saying of it, since to me it is the truth. Art, I suppose, you think of as the realm and privilege of selected men, of sculptors, painters, musicians, poets, men of genius and having something that has always been called divine in their faculty; but it appears to me that art, like genius, is something that all men share, that it is the stamp of the soul in every one, and constitutes their true and immaterial life. The soul of the race, as it is seen in history and disclosed by history, is an artist soul; its career is an artistic career; its unerring selective power expels from its memory every mortal element and perserves only the essential spirit, and thereof builds its ideal imaginative world through which it finds its true expression; its more perfect comprehension of the world is science, its more perfect comprehension of its own nature is love, its more perfect expression of its remembered life is art. Mankind is the grandest and surest artist of all, and history as it clarifies is, in pure fact, an artistic process, a creation in its fullness of the beautiful soul.

It appears, then, that the language of literature in the race is a perfected nature and a perfected manhood and a perfected divinity, so far as the race at the moment can see toward perfection. The life which literature builds up ideally out of the material of experience is not wholly a past life, but there mingles with it and at last controls it the life that man desires to live. Fullness of life — that fullness of action which is poured in the epic, that fullness of passion which is poured in the drama, that fullness of desire that is poured in the lyric — the life of which man knows himself capable and realizes as the opportunity and hope of life — this is the life that literature enthrones in its dream. You have heard much of the will to believe and of the desire to live: literature is made of these two, warp and woof. Race after race believes in the gods it has come to know and in the heroes it has borne, and in what it wishes to believe of divine and human experience; and the life it thus ascribes to its gods and to its own past is the life it most ardently desires to live. Literature, which records this, is thus the chief witness to the nobility, the constancy and instancy of man's effort for perfection. What wonder, then, if in his sublimest and tenderest song there steals that note of melancholy so often struck by the greatest masters in the crisis and climax of their works, and which, when so struck, has more of the infinite in it, more of the human in it, than any other in the slowly triumphant theme!

To sum up — the language of literature is experience; the language of race-literature is race-experience, or history, the human use that the race has made of the world. The law appears to be that history in this sense is slowly transformed by a refining and spiritualizing process into an imaginative world, such as the world of mythology, chivalry or the Scriptures, and that this world in turn becomes emblematic and fades away into an expression of abstract truth. The crude beginning of the process is seen in our historical fiction; the height of it in Arthur or in Odin; the end of it in the symbolic or allegoric interpretation of even so human a book as Virgil's "Aeneid." Human desire for the best enters into this process with such force that the record of the past slowly changes into the prophecy of the future, and out of the passing away of what was is built the dream of what shall be; so arises in race-life the creed of what man wishes to believe and the dream of the life he desires to live; this human desire for belief and for life is, in the final analysis, the principle of selection whose operation has been sketched, and on its validity rests the validity and truth of all literature.

The Torch

III

THE TITAN MYTH

I

I propose to-night to illustrate by the specific example of the Titan Myth how it is that Greek mythology is a tongue of the imagination — a living tongue of the universal imagination of men.

The Titan Myth — I wonder what it means to you? The Titans were the earliest children of the earth, elder than the Greek gods even, and were the sons of the the Earth, their mother. You perhaps think of them as mere giants, such as Jack killed -- mediæval monsters of the kin of Beauty and the Beast. Think of them rather as majestic forms, with something of the sweep and mystery of those figures you may remember out of Ossian and his misty mountains, with the largeness and darkness of the earth in them, a massive dim-featured race, but with an earthly rather than celestial grandeur, embodiments of mighty force dull to beauty, intelligence, light. When Zeus, the then young Olympian, was born, and with him the other deities of the then new divine world and when he dethroned his father, and put the new gods in possession of the universe, these children of the old regimé, misliking change, took the father's part, and warred on the usurper of ancient power, and were overthrown by his lightnings, and mountains were piled on them; and now you may read in Longfellow of Enceladus, the type and image of their fate, buried under Ætna whose earthquakes are the struggling of the great Titan beneath. This was the war of the Titans and the gods. One of the Titans, however, stood apart from the rest, being wiser than they. Prometheus made friends with Zeus, but his fortune was not less grievous to him; for when he saw that Zeus took no account of men — "of miserable men," but yearned to destroy them from the face of the earth, he took pity on mankind, and stole for them the celestial fire and gave it to them, for until then man had lived a life of mere nature, without knowledge, or any arts, not even that of agriculture. Prometheus was the fire-bringer; and, bringing fire, he brought to men all the uses of fire, such as metal-working, for example, and in a word he gave to mankind its entire career, the long labour of progressive civilization, and the life of the spirit itself which is kindled, as we say, from the Promethean spark within. It was but a step for the Pagan imagination, at a later stage, to think of this patron of mankind as the creator of men, since he was the fosterer of their lives; it was said that he had made clay images, and moistened these with holy water, so that they became living creatures — men. Zeus was angered by this befriending of the human race; and he flung Prometheus upon a mountain of the Caucasus, chained him there, and planted a vulture to eat always on his entrails; and in the imagination of men there he hangs to this day. Yet there was one condition on which he might be released and again received into heaven. He alone knew the secret of the fall of Zeus — the means by which it would be brought about; and if he would tell this secret, so that Zeus might avoid the danger as was possible, and thereby his unjust reign become perpetual, Prometheus might save himself. But the Titan so loved justice that he kept silence, knowing that in the course of ages at last Zeus would fall. This was the myth of Prometheus.

Of the aspects which the entire legend presents in literature, there are three which stand out. I shall ask you to consider the first as the cosmic idea — the idea of the law of human progress that it contains. To the Greek mind the development of the universe consisted in the supplanting of a lower by a higher power, under the will of a supreme fate or necessity which was above both gods and men: after Uranus was Chronos, after Chronos was Zeus, after Zeus there would be other gods. The

Greeks were themselves a higher power in their world, and as such had conquered the Persians; theirs was the victory of light over darkness, of civilization over barbarism, and therefore on the walls of their great temple, the Parthenon, which was the embodiment of their spiritualeconsciousness as a race, they depicted three great mythic events symbolizing the victory of the higher power — that is, the war of the Centaurs and the Lapithæ, of the Athenians and the Amazons, and of the gods and the Titans. This cosmic idea — the Greek conception of progress — it is more convenient to delay to the next lecture. Secondly, I shall ask you to consider the conception of the friend of man suffering for his sake — one that without irreverence may be designated as the Christ-idea. This phase of the myth naturally has received less development in literature, inasmuch as the ideas and emotions it embodies find expression inevitably and almost exclusively in the symbol of the Cross and the life that led up thereto. But for those who, in the chances of time have stood apart from the established faith of Christendom, and have not seldom encountered the creed and practice of their age in persecution, being victims for the sake of reason — for these men, the figure of Prometheus has been in the place of the Cross, an image of themselves, their prototype. The expression of this particular idea, however, has been slight in literature; but it naturally appears there, and Prometheus has come to be the characteristic symbol of the peculiar suffering of genius; so Longfellow uses it in his "Prometheus."

> "*All is but a symbol painted*
> *Of the Poet, Prophet, Seer;*
> *Only those are crowned and sainted*
> *Who with grief have been acquainted,*
> *Making nations nobler, freer.*"

Under this aspect Prometheus is the martyr of humanity. Thirdly, I shall ask you to consider the conception of Prometheus, not as an individual, but as identified with mankind, as mankind itself suffering in all its race-life and throughout its history, wretched, tyrannized over by some dark and unjust necessity, yet unterrified, resolute, invincible in its faith in that

> "*One far-off divine event*
> *To which the whole creation moves.*"

The imagination, age after age, finds in Prometheus such a symbol of man's race-life. This is to conceive of Prometheus as the idea of humanity.

Æschylus fixed the form of the Titan for the imagination and surrounded it with the characteristic scene. He nailed Prometheus in chains riveted into the rock, the vast desolate cliffs of the Caucasus, an indistinct and mighty figure, frosted with the night and watching the stars in their courses with lidless eyes, the dark vulture hovering in his bosom. Perhaps I can make the scene more real to you by a passage from a letter of a friend who last spring was in that solitude. "All the forenoon," he says, "I have been travelling forward beneath the giant wall of the frosty Caucasus. The snow-clad plain serves as a dazzling foreground to the towering rugged peaks so sharply defined in steel white and dull black wherever the snow leaves the beetling rock bare. The gorges and ravines which are here and there visible look like old-time scars of jagged wounds on the sullen face of the mountains. The dreary solitude of the scene is very impressive. Far off yonder in the distance I can picture the chill and desolate vulture-peak where Prometheus, in his galling chains, longed for the day to give peace to 'starry-kirtled night' (if I remember my Æschylus rightly) and yearned for the sun to arise and dispell the hoar-frost of dawn. It all comes up again before my mind in this far-away solitary region." Thither to this scene, that my friend describes, came with comfort or counsel the daughters of the Ocean, and old Oceanus himself, the Titan's brother, and Io on her wanderings, and Hermes, the messenger of Zeus, to make terms with Prometheus, or to inflict new tortures should he refuse.

But Prometheus remained the resolute and faithful sufferer: there stretched on the rock he would await the sure coming of that justice which is above even the heavens of Zeus and contains and orders even them. It is a sublime moral situation. Who could ever forget that figure, once stamped on his imagination, though but a schoolboy? So Byron remembered his Harrow days: "Of the 'Prometheus' of Æschylus," he says: "I was passionately fond as a boy. It was one of the Greek dramas we used to read three times a year at Harrow. Indeed, it and the Medea were the only ones, except the 'Seven Against Thebes,' which pleased me. The 'Prometheus,' if not exactly in my plan has always been so much in my head that I well understand how its influences have passed into all I have done." It goes with this acknowledgment, and bespeaks the critic's acute penetration, to find Jeffrey affirming that there is no work of modern literature that more than Byron's "Manfred" approaches the "Prometheus" of Æschylus. Byron only illustrates the fascination that this myth has for the race; the world will never let go of this symbol of itself.

The moment and the cause, the invincible resolution denying the will of the apparent gods of the hour in obedience to the higher light within, are the same that have nailed all martyrs to the cross, sent patriots to rot in prisons, and borne on the leaders of all forlorn hopes in their death-charges, and of these the history of the last century gives many a modern instance. In our own time Siberia has been one vast Caucasus; I remember when not long ago its name was Crete; and now 't is Macedonia — they are all tracts of that desolation that swallows up in its voiceless solitude and buries from the ears of God and man the human cry. In the mind and memory of the race there are two great mountains; over against Sinai towers the peak of the Caucasus with perpetual challenge; yet they are twin peaks — one, the mount of faith in God, the other, the mount of faith in man. You know how the race, from time to time, as great moods sweep over it — the mood of asceticism, or of Christian chivalry, or of world-conquest, sets up some historic figure as the type and expression of this mood — some St. Francis, or Philip Sidney, or Napoleon; this is because the race sees in these men a greater image of itself in those particular moods. So, in a more abstract way the race takes some part of its self-consciousness — say, its perception of what is evil in its own heart — and puts it outside of itself so as to see it better, projects or objectifies itself, as we say, in an image, like Mephistopheles; it sees in Mephistopheles itself in a certain mood — a mood of mocking denial of all good. So, in its own history and memory the race perceives that often its greatest men, those who have been its civilizers, have been victims of the powers of their day, and have served the race and carried on its life by fidelity to their own hearts and the truth in them in spite of the utmost suffering that could be inflicted on them. The race thinks of these men as constituting its own life, gathers and blends them in one being and finds that being — the type that stands for its continuous life — in Prometheus. In him the race projects — as I have said — or objectifies itself in the mood of suffering the worst for the good of men, with undismayed courage and unbroken will. Prometheus is man as he knows himself in history, the immortal sufferer under injustice bringing even by his sorrows the higher justice that shall at last prevail — he is this figure set clear and separate before the mind: he is the idea of humanity, conceived in the characteristic act of its noblest life — he is mankind.

I dwelt in the last lecture on the treasure that the race-imagination possesses in the Greek myths, as a means of expression; in the whole inheritance of our literature there is nothing that the poet finds so great a gift as these forms and tales of the mythic world in which the work of creation is already half done for him, and the storing of ideas and emotions has been accomplished, so that with a word he can release in the mind the flood of meaning they contain, as if he pushed an electric button; they are to him what the common law is to a lawyer — the stored results of the past, in experience and principle; he has only to adopt them into his human verse, as he adopts into his verse of nature the Andes and Ararat. It was not surprising that such a tale as the Titan Myth should be among the chief memories of the race, never wholly forgotten; yet it waited for its moment. After the first mention of it in literature three thousand years went by, before the moment came. Then the French Revolution struck its hour. It is true that the myth stirred in the Renaissance when all things Greek revived, and Calderon, the great Spanish poet, treated some minor aspects of it; but, in and about the Revolution, it was handled repeatedly by great poets who strove to recast the story and use it to express the ideas and emotions of their own age. Goethe in his youth, and the Germans — Herder and Schlegel, each wrote a Prometheus; in Italy Monti took the subject; in England Landor and Byron touched it lightly, and Keats and Shelley made it the matter of great poems; and later, in France, where Voltaire had approached it, Victor Hugo and Edgar Quinet elaborated it; nor do these names exhaust the list of those who in the last century made it a principal theme of verse. This re-birth was a natural one; for the French Revolution, which you remember Wendell

Phillips in his great Harvard speech described as "the most unmixed blessing that ever befell mankind" — the French Revolution was rooted in the idea of humanity and was the cause of humanity. Moreover, the Revolution has a Titanic quality in itself; there is the feeling of large earth-might in the struggle of the heavy masses of the darkened people, peasant-born; and in their revolt against the kingdoms of the world whose serfs they were, there was the sense of a strife with the careless luxury of the unjust gods; there was in the wretchedness of the European peoples the state of man that Prometheus pitied when he rebuked Zeus for taking no account of men — "of miserable men;" and in the tumult and ardour and invincible faith of the Revolution there was both the Titanic atmosphere and the Promethean spirit. Shelley was the poet through whom the literary expression of the Revolution was to be poured. It is necessary to mark the time precisely. The Revolution had flamed, and in Napoleon, whom more than one poet celebrated as the Prometheus of the age, had apparently flamed out. The Revolution, as a political idea seemed to have failed, and Europe sank back into the arms of king and priest. It was then that these great Englishmen, Byron and Shelley, in their youth took up the fallen cause and bore it onward in their hands till Byron died for it in the war of Greek Independence and Shelley, having sung his song, sank in the waters of the Mediterranean Sea.

Shelley came to this subject naturally and through years of unconscious preparation; and when the moment of creation came, he felt the Titanic quality, that I spoke of, in the Revolution, felt the Promethean security of victory it contained — felt, too, the Promethean suffering which was the heart of mankind as he saw it surveying Europe in his day, and knew it in his own bosom as well. He conceived of Prometheus as mankind, of his history and fate as the destiny of man; and being full of that far sight of Prometheus which saw the victorious send — being as full of it as the wheel of Ezekiel was full of eyes — he saw, as the centre of all vision, Prometheus Unbound — the millennium of mankind. He imagined the process of that great liberation and its crowning prosperities. This is his poem. In this poem the Revolution as a moral idea reached its height; that is what makes it, from the social point of view, the race-point of view, the greatest work of the last century in creative imagination — for it is the summary and centre, in the world of art, of the greatest power in that century — the power of the idea of humanity. I shall present only the cardinal phases of the dramatic situation, in the poem, and of the moral idea by which it is solved.

The poem opens in the Caucasus, with Prometheus

bound to the rock, an indistinct figure such as I have described him; his form is left undefined — he is a voice in the vast solitudes; and his first speech, which discloses the situation, makes you aware of physical suffering, mental anguish, an undismayed and patient will, an unconquerable faith — these are the qualities which make him an elemental being and characterize him at once. It is an Æschylean speech, phrases from Æschylus are welded into it; but the moral grandeur of Prometheus — all, that is, except the historical and physical features of the scene — bears the creative mark of Shelley's own sublimity of conception.

"*Monarch of Gods and Daemons, and all Spirits*
But One, who throng those bright and rolling worlds
Which Thou and I alone of living things
Behold with sleepless eyes! regard this Earth
Made multitudinous with thy slaves, whom thou
Requitest for knee-worship, prayer, and praise,
And toil, and hecatombs of broken hearts,
With fear and self-contempt and barren hope.
Whilst me, who am thy foe, eyeless in hate,
Hast thou made reign and triumph, to thy scorn
O'er mine own misery and thy vain revenge.
Three thousand years of sleep-unsheltered hours,
And moments aye divided by keen pangs
Till they seemed years, torture and solitude,
Scorn and despair, — these are mine empire: —

More glorious far than that which thou surveyest
From thine unenvied throne, O, Mighty God!
Almighty, had I deigned to share the shame
Of thine ill tyranny, and hung not here
Nailed to this wall of eagle-baffling mountain,
Black, wintry, dead, unmeasured; without herb,
Insect, or beast, or shape or sound of life.
Ah me! alas, pain, pain ever, for ever!

"*No change, no pause, no hope! Yet I endure.*
I ask the Earth, have not the mountains felt?
I ask yon Heaven, the all-beholding Sun,
Has it not seen? The Sea, in storm or calm,
Heaven's ever-changing Shadow, spread below,
Have its deaf waves not heard my agony?
Ah me! alas, pain, pain ever, for ever!

"*The crawling glaciers pierce me with the spears*
Of their moon-freezing crystals, the bright chains
Eat with their burning cold into my bones.
Heaven's wingèd hound, polluting from thy lips
His beak in poison not his own, tears up
My heart; and shapeless sights come wandering by,
The ghastly people of the realm of dream,
Mocking me: and the Earthquake-fiends are charged
To wrench the rivets from my quivering wounds
When the rocks split and close again behind:
While from their loud abysses howling throng
The genii of the storm, urging the rage
Of whirlwind, and afflict me with keen hail.

And yet to me welcome is day and night,
Whether one breaks the hoar frost of the morn,
Or starry, dim, and slow, the other climbs
The leaden-coloured east; for then they lead
The wingless, crawling hours, one among whom
— As some dark Priest hales the reluctant victim —
Shall drag thee, cruel King, to kiss the blood
From these pale feet, which then might trample thee
If they disdained not such a prostrate slave.
Disdain! Ah no! I pity thee. What ruin
Will hunt thee undefended through the wide Heaven!
How will thy soul, cloven to its depth with terror,
Gape like a hell within! I speak in grief
Not exultation, for I hate no more,
As then ere misery made me wise. The curse
Once breathed on thee I would recall. Ye Mountains,
Whose many-voiced Echoes, through the mist
Of cataracts, flung the thunder of that spell!
Ye icy Springs, stagnant with wrinkling frost,
Which vibrated to hear me, and then crept
Shuddering through India! Thou serenest Air,
Through which the Sun walks burning without beams!
And ye swift Whirlwinds, who on poised wings
Hung mute and moveless o'er yon hushèd abyss,
As thunder, louder than your own, made rock
The orbèd world! If then my words had power,
Though I am changed so that aught evil wish
Is dead within; although no memory be
Of what is hate, let them not lose it now!
What was that curse? for ye all heard me speak."

Prometheus's character, you observe, is developed in the point that he no longer hates Zeus, but is filled with pity for him. Later in the scene the Furies enter, to torture the Titan with new torments. What torments will be the most piercing to the suffering spirit of man — the spirit that suffers in advancing human welfare? Will it not be the fact that the gifts he has given man have proved evil gifts, and that in the effort for perfection man has but the more heaped on himself damnation? The thought is found in many treatments of the myth: Themis warned Prometheus that in aiding man with fire and the arts he only increased man's woes. It is the old pessimistic thought that civilization is a curse — that the only growth of the soul is growth in the capacity for pain, for disillusion, for despair. Shelley introduces it in quite the Promethean spirit — as a thing, which if it be, is to be borne. What were the two characteristic failures of human hope in Shelley's eyes? The capital instances? They were the failure of Christianity to bring the millennium, and the failure of the French Revolution in the same end — and not only their failure to bring the millennium, but, on the contrary, their influence in still further confounding the state of mankind and flooding the nations with new miseries. The Furies show these two failures to Prometheus in vision. The passage is somewhat involved as the vision is successively disclosed through the words of the chorus of Furies, of the attendant sisters Ione and Panthea, and of Prometheus, but I will endeavour to make it plain:

" Chorus

" *The pale stars of the morn*
Shine on a misery, dire to be borne.
Dost thou faint, mighty Titan? We laugh thee to scorn.
Dost thou boast the clear knowledge thou waken'dst for man?
Then was kindled within him a thirst which outran
Those perishing waters; a thirst of fierce fever,
Hope, love, doubt, desire, which consume him for ever
One came forth of gentle worth
Smiling on the sanguine earth;
His words outlived him, like swift poison
Withering up truth, peace, and pity.
Look! where round the wide horizon
Many a million-peopled city
Vomits smoke in the bright air.
Mark that outcry of despair!
'T is his mild and gentle ghost
Wailing for the faith he kindled:
Look again, the flames almost
To a glow-worm's lamp have dwindled:
The survivors round the embers
Gather in dread.
Joy, joy, joy!
Past ages crowd on thee, but each one remembers,
And the future is dark, and the present is spread
Like a pillow of thorns for thy slumberless head.

"SEMICHORUS I

"Drops of bloody agony flow
From his white and quivering brow.
Grant a little respite now:
See a disenchanted nation
Springs like day from desolation;
To Truth its state is dedicate,
And Freedom leads it forth, her mate;
A legioned band of linkèd brothers
Whom Love calls children —

"SEMICHORUS II

"'*T is another's:*
See how kindred murder kin:
'T is the vintage time for death and sin:
Blood, like new wine, bubbles within:
Till Despair smothers
The struggling world, which slaves and tyrants win.
[ALL THE FURIES VANISH, EXCEPT ONE]
IONE. *Hark, sister! what a low yet dreadful groan*
Quite unsuppressed is tearing up the heart
Of the good Titan, as storms tear the deep,
And beasts hear the sea moan in inland caves.
Darest thou observe how the fiends torture him?
PANTHEA. *Alas! I looked forth twice, but will no more.*
IONE. *What didst thou see?*
PANTHEA. *A woful sight: a youth*
With patient looks nailed to a crucifix.
IONE. *What next?*

PANTHEA. *The heaven around, the earth below*
Was peopled with thick shapes of human death,
All horrible, and wrought by human hands,
And some appeared the work of human hearts,
For men were slowly killed by frowns and smiles:
And other sights too foul to speak and live
Were wandering by. Let us not tempt worse fear
By looking forth: those groans are grief enough.
FURY. *Behold an emblem: those who do endure*
Deep wrongs for man, and scorn, and chains, but heap
Thousandfold torment on themselves and him.
PROMETHEUS. *Remit the anguish of that lighted stare;*
Close those wan lips; let that thorn-wounded brow
Stream not with blood; it mingles with thy tears!
Fix, fix those tortured orbs in peace and death,
So thy sick throes shake not that crucifix,
So those pale fingers play not with thy gore.
O, horrible! Thy name I will not speak,
It hath become a curse. I see, I see
The wise, the mild, the lofty, and the just,
Whom thy slaves hate for being like to thee,
Some hunted by foul lies from their heart's home,
An early-chosen, late-lamented home;
As hooded ounces cling to the driven hind;
Some linked to corpses in unwholesome cells:
Some — Hear I not the multitude laugh loud? —
Impaled in lingering fire: and mighty realms
Float by my feet, like sea-uprooted isles,
Whose sons are kneaded down in common blood
By the red light of their own burning homes.

FURY. *Blood thou canst see, and fire; and canst hear groans;*
Worse things, unheard, unseen, remain behind.
PROMETHEUS. *Worse?*
FURY. *In each human heart terror survives*
The ruin it has gorged: the loftiest fear
All that they would disdain to think were true:
Hypocrisy and custom make their minds
The fanes of many a worship, now outworn.
They dare not devise good for man's estate,
And yet they know not that they do not dare.
The good want power, but to weep barren tears.
The powerful goodness want: worse need for them.
The wise want love; and those who love want wisdom;
And all best things are thus confused to ill.
Many are strong and rich, and would be just,
But live among their suffering fellow-men
As if none felt: they know not what they do.
PROMETHEUS. *Thy words are like a cloud of wingèd snakes;*
And yet I pity those they torture not.
FURY. *Thou pitiest them? I speak no more!* [VANISHES]
PROMETHEUS. *Ah woe!*
Ah woe! Alas! pain, pain ever, for ever!
I close my tearless eyes, but see more clear
Thy works within my woe-illumèd mind,
Thou subtle tyrant! Peace is in the grave.
The grave hides all things beautiful and good:
I am a God and cannot find it there,
Nor would I seek it: for, though dread revenge,
This is defeat, fierce king, not victory.
The sights with which thou torturest gird my soul

With new endurance, till the hour arrives
When they shall be no types of things which are.
PANTHEA. *Alas! what sawest thou?*
PROMETHEUS. *There are two woes:*
To speak, and to behold; thou spare me one.
Names are there, Nature's sacred watchwords, they
Were borne aloft in bright emblazonry;
The nations thronged around, and cried aloud,
As with one voice, Truth, liberty, and love!
Suddenly fierce confusion fell from heaven
Among them: there was strife, deceit, and fear.
Tyrants rushed in, and did divide the spoil.
This was the shadow of the truth I saw."

The victory of Prometheus is in his declaration that he pities those who are not tortured by such scenes. He had already disclosed this pitiful heart in his first speech; and, desiring to hear the curse he had originally launched on Zeus, and being gratified in this wish by the Earth, he had revoked it:

> " *It doth repent me: words are quick and vain;*
> *Grief for awhile is blind, and so was mine.*
> *I wish no living thing to suffer pain.*"

Thus he had forgiven his great enemy.

As I read the play, this forgiveness of Zeus by Prometheus makes the predestined hour of the downfall of Zeus. The chariot bears aloft the new principle of supreme being, a higher and younger-born principle, which exceeds that which Zeus embodied, just as Zeus had in his birth been a higher principle than the old reign contained; and Zeus is flung headlong, like Lucifer, into the abyss of past things. Thus Shelley, as is the universal way of genius, had created a great work by fusing in it two divergent products of the human spirit — the Hellenic idea of a higher power superseding the lower, and the Christian idea that this power was one of non-resistance, of forgiveness, of love. The reign of love now begins in the poem: Prometheus is released and wedded with Asia, who stands for the spirit of nature, in which marriage is typified the union of the human soul with nature, the harmony of man and nature, and he shares in the millennium which is thus established on earth.

At the end, you observe, the Titan Myth drops away; it does not appear in the last acts; for in it there was no such completion of the Promethean faith as Shelley describes.

And here I might end the discussion of Shelley's handling of the myth; but I cannot refrain from directing your attention to the marvellous power of the myth which could so blend the Greek and Christian genius, and contain the passion of the French Revolution issuing in the highest and most extreme forms of Chris-

THE TITAN MYTH

II

The importance of history in literature can hardly be emphasized too much. I have not hesitated to speak of mythology and chivalry, and even of the Scriptures, as transformations of history, and of imaginative literature as the spiritual after-life both of historical events and conditions in the narrow sense, and of general human experience in the broad sense. I have directed attention also to the influence of history in a more direct way, in the literature of the last century — to its inspirational power there; out of it came, in particular, the picturesqueness of the historical novel; and, inasmuch as the romantic spirit of the century explored all lands and times for new material, and eagerly absorbed all that travel or research brought forward new to the European mind, it naturally happened that the conception of historical humanity became one of rich variety; the formula —" many men, many minds "— received unending illustration, and it might be thought that the result would have been to impress on the race a sense of hopeless diversity in its members rather than of unbroken unity. But history had this inspirational power, not only in literature, but in philosophy; the mind of man was stimulated to find in all this new mass of different detail a single principle that would explain and reconcile the apparent confusion — to frame, that is, a philosophy of history. Herder, the German writer, was one of the most influential of the great men who attacked this problem; he gave his life to it. At the dawn of a new age, you know, there is often a singular phenomenon: men of genius arise, with a poetical cast of mind, and they are prophetic of the new day because they show forth some single idea or mood of it though they do not grasp the whole; they catch like morning clouds, some the red, some the gold, some the purple ray, but none of them gives that one white light which will prevail when the day is fully come. An outburst of poetry — the prevalence of a poetical view of things — is the sign of an advance along the whole line. Herder was a man of this kind; and it is easy now to say that his method was imperfectly scientific, and that his imagination and desire led him astray. Nevertheless he had one of those minds which, if it does not build a system squared of solid timber, flings seeds on every wind like a living tree. His intellect was capacious, and in the attempt he made to include all things in his philosophizing he seems an anticipation of Herbert Spencer; in his theorizing, too, students find innumerable thoughts — that are half-guesses — which are almost the words of Darwin. He was, thus, you see, in the true path of advance; he caught the first gleams of the new hour of time. He was interested, over and above all else, in humanity and its destiny as disclosed in history. He saw in history the working of a law of beneficence and justice, which though it might not seem such when viewed in its means, always and unfailingly is such when viewed in its end; thus from the concourse and struggle of forces in civilization there is always issuing the slow triumph of reason. This was what Herder conceived as the law of progress; and is the view taken in his leading prose works, the "Ideas on the History of Mankind" and the "Letters for the Furtherance of Humanity," which are still great and fruitful books. At the very end of a life spent thus in meditation on the career of man in civilization, Herder set forth his faith in the principle of progress in a series of dramatic scenes built out of the myth of Prometheus. He identified the fire which was the Titan's characteristic gift to mortals, as civilization, and saw in it the two-fold symbol — first, of the arts themselves, secondly, of that divine soul which restlessly excites and spurs on all the powers of man.

I will sketch very briefly the story as Herder tells it. Prometheus has been long chained to the rock, and (as in Shelley's poem) time has ripened and softened his heart, partly because he knows that his work is prospering among men. In the first scene he hears a distant song of victory, and voices announce to him that reason fructifies the earth. In later scenes, first the daughters of the Ocean and old Oceanus himself come complaining that mankind disturbs the sea with ships, changes the course of the waters by dams and canals, and brings the ends of the earth together with commerce; but Prometheus replies, prophesying: —

"*The sea which girds the earth shall be the mediator and peace-maker of the nations.*"

Then the Dryads, daughters of the earth come, with a similar tale; but Prometheus tells them that in the end man will make a garden of the earth; and other mythological characters enter, each with its tale, Ceres, the goddess of harvest, who works with man — and Bacchus, the giver of the vine: at last Hercules and Theseus release the Titan, all go before Themis, the goddess of justice who judges the cause between Prometheus and the gods, and gives the decision for Prometheus. Pallas then leads to Prometheus Agatia, the pure spirit of humanity, and the drama ends. You see the work is little more than a series of picturesque classical tableaux, in which the victory of man through reason is set forth with a maintenance of self-sacrifice, perseverance, patience, social labour and love as the essential elements of the moral ideal.

A few years before, Schlegel had produced a Prometheus in the form of a poem, in the same realm of history but with much less scenic elaboration. In it he describes the Golden Age before the Titan War, the desolate state of man after Zeus came to the throne, and how Prometheus made of clay a new race, and animated the clay with the heavenly fire. Themis reproves him for this act, and foretells the sorrows of this Promethean man — this being of divine desire chained to the earth and tyrannized over by the thought of the past and of the future alike. But Prometheus believes, he says, that good will not die, that the toil of one generation will help the next, that human will reduces life to order and human action subdues nature; and that out of the midst of opposing principles civilization grows to more and more. The law of progress is stated with sure optimism: though there may be ages of terror and apparent degeneration, yet the immortal principle of good in the race is such that it passes invulnerable through all history, and accomplishes the work of civilization. The poem is no more than a reply to the sad prophecy of

Themis, and perhaps incidentally to such reactionaries as saw in the Reign of Terror and the Revolution generally the denial of progress and of the social ideal.

But in the sphere of history, one of the latest reworkings of the myth, the Prometheus of Quinet, the French poet, contains the most interesting variation. He conceived firmly the unity of history; and in obedience to this conception he endeavoured to unite the Greek myth with Christianity, not ethically as Shelley did, but historically. "If Prometheus" — he says in his preface — "is the eternal prophet, as his name indicates, each new age of humanity can put new oracles in the mouth of the Titan. Perhaps there is no character so well fitted to express the feelings — the premature and half melancholy desires — in which our age is enchained." In this spirit he wrote a drama in three parts: the first depicts the creation of man by Prometheus, the gift of fire — that is, the soul — and the beginning of life in sorrow. The second part depicts the suffering of Prometheus on Caucasus, in which the foreknowledge of the fall of Zeus becomes a prophecy of Christ's coming. The third act depicts the advent of Christianity. The Archangels, Raphael and Michael descend on Caucasus, and release Prometheus, who rises transfigured; the gods of Olympus prostrate themselves before him and the angels, and pray in vain for life. Then Prometheus has a singular thought which to me is the most dramatic in the play: as he listens to the death-song of the gods, his mind is clouded with a doubt: — will not the new divinity also pass away? — and does he not already see a new Caucasus before him in the distant time? — will he not be bound again? — The angels comfort him, and he ascends to heaven; but as he disappears in that hierarchy of celestial peace and love, he still wears the shadow of thought — for he remembers that on earth men still suffer. This attempt at a true synthesis of the Greek and Christian imagination — in behalf of the unity of history — is a most interesting illustration of the spirit of the century; which was on the whole a century of peace-making between the great historic elements of spiritual civilization, a drawing together and harmonizing of religions, philosophies and half-developed and fragmentary doctrines, by virtue of the identical principle they contain; or as Herder said, in consequence of that symmetry of human reason which makes all nobler minds tend to think the same thoughts.

Interesting as the historical point of view is, it is plain that the myth loses something of its poetical quality, becomes pure allegory, becomes almost mechanical; it becomes, in fact, what is called poetical machinery, a hard and fast means of figurative expression. The characters in Herder and Schlegel move like marionettes, and you hear the voice of the author apart from his work. Let us turn to a mind in which the myth really was alive again, with creative as well as expressive power — the mind of Keats. In his "Hyperion," the tale is of the Titans immediately after their overthrow; they have been dethroned from power, Saturn is an exile hiding in the deep glens, but their ruin is still incomplete; Hyperion still is lord in the sun, and the others are at liberty to gather for a great council. In order to display the idea of Keats, let me approach it indirectly. The point of view which he takes has much affinity with science — more, that is, than with either history or ethics. Modern theories of evolution have accustomed our minds to the conception of an original state of the universe, vast, homogeneous, undiversified, simple; out of this — to adopt the nebular theory — slowly great masses conglomerated, gathered into sun and planets; and out of these arose finally living things on a smaller scale but of higher perfection of being. Now if you will think of man's progressive conceptions of the divinity as something similar to this, as parallel to it, you will have Keats's idea. In the beginning were the vast, vague, undefined, half-unconscious beings, like Uranus, the heavens, and Gaia, the earth, and Chronos, time; to them succeeded the more conscious and half-humanized brood of the Titans, like the sun and planets, as it were; last came the gods of Olympus, in the perfection of full humanity, and on the physical scale of man in form, feature and spirit. The change from the Titanic to the Olympian rule, was like the change from one geological age of vast forms of brute and vegetable life to another of smaller but nobler species. The higher principle displaces the lower, according to that Greek idea of progress which I have described; and this successive displacement of the lower by the higher is the law of development in the Universe.

In Keats's poem, Oceanus, speaking to the Titans in council as the wisest of them all, sets forth the matter plainly, and I should like you to notice how the conception of a progressive order in nature (not as hitherto in civilization merely) and the conception of the necessity of accepting truth, bear the mark of the scientific spirit. Oceanus thus speaks: —

> " *We fall by course of Nature's law, not force*
> *Of thunder, or of Jove. Great Saturn, thou*
> *Hast sifted well the atom-universe;*
> *But for this reason, that thou art the King,*
> *And only blind from sheer supremacy,*
> *One avenue was shaded from thine eyes,*
> *Through which I wander'd to eternal truth.*
> *And first, as thou wast not the first of powers,*

So art thou not the last; it cannot be;
Thou art not the beginning nor the end.
From chaos and parental darkness came
Light, the first fruits of that intestine broil,
That sullen ferment, which for wondrous ends
Was ripening in itself. The ripe hour came,
And with it light, and light engendering
Upon its own producer, forthwith touch'd
The whole enormous matter into life.
Upon that very hour, our parentage,
The Heavens and the Earth, were manifest:
Then thou first-born, and we the giant-race,
Found ourselves ruling new and beauteous realms.
Now comes the pain of truth, to whom 't is pain;
O folly! for to bear all naked truths,
And to envisage circumstance, all calm,
That is the top of sovereignty. Mark well!
As Heaven and Earth are fairer, fairer far
Than Chaos and blank Darkness, though once chiefs;
And as we show beyond that Heaven and Earth
In form and shape compact and beautiful,
In will, in action free, companionship,
And thousand other signs of purer life;
So on our heels a fresh perfection treads,
A power more strong in beauty, born of us
And fated to excel us, as we pass
In glory that old Darkness: nor are we
Thereby more conquer'd, than by us the rule
Of shapeless Chaos. Say, doth the dull soil
Quarrel with the proud forests it hath fed

And feedeth still, more comely than itself?
Can it deny the chiefdom of green groves?
Or shall the tree be envious of the dove
Because it cooeth, and hath snowy wings
To wander wherewithal and find its joys?
We are such forest-trees, and our fair boughs
Have bared forth, not pale solitary doves,
But eagles golden-feather'd, who do tower
Above us in their beauty, and must reign
In right thereof; for 't is the eternal law
That first in beauty should be first in might:
Yea, by that law, another race may drive
Our conquerors to mourn as we do now.
Have ye beheld the young God of the Seas,
My dispossessor? Have ye seen his face?
Have ye beheld his chariot, foam'd along
By noble wingèd creatures he hath made?
I saw him on the calmed waters scud,
With such a glow of beauty in his eyes,
That it enforced me to bid sad farewell
To all my empire; farewell sad I took,
And hither came, to see how dolorous fate
Had wrought upon ye; and how I might best
Give consolation in this woe extreme.
Receive the truth, and let it be your balm."

It appears, then, that the new principle of being, in whose advent lay the ruin of the old world, is beauty.

"'T is the eternal law
That first in beauty should be first in might."

This is, as you know, Keats's distinctive mark — the perception and adoration of beauty. What love was to Shelley, that beauty was to Keats — the open door to divinity; he saw life as a form of beauty. And he means what he says — not that beauty has strength as an added quality, but that beauty is strength, and reigns in its own right. This rise of the Olympians was beauty's moment of birth in the minds of men; this birth was a revelation, like a new religion, and it is presented as such by Keats in a two-fold way. First it is a revelation to the Titans. You have seen how Oceanus on beholding the new god of the sea, gave up the rule over it. So Clymene, who describes herself —

"O Father, I am here the simplest voice" —

tells her experience:

" I stood upon a shore, a pleasant shore,
Where a sweet clime was breathèd from a land
Of fragrance, quietness, and trees, and flowers.
Full of calm joy it was, as I of grief;
Too full of joy and soft delicious warmth;
So that I felt a movement in my heart
To chide, and to reproach that solitude
With songs of misery, music of our woes;
And sat me down, and took a mouthèd shell
And murmur'd into it, and made melody —
O melody no more! for while I sang,

And with poor skill let pass into the breeze
The dull shell's echo, from a bowery strand
Just opposite, an island of the sea,
There came enchantment with the shifting wind,
That did both drown and keep alive my ears.
I threw my shell away upon the sand,
And a wave fill'd it, as my sense was fill'd
With that new blissful golden melody.
A living death was in each gush of sounds,
Each family of rapturous hurried notes,
That fell, one after one, yet all at once,
Like pearl beads dropping sudden from their string:
And then another, then another strain,
Each like a dove leaving its olive perch,
With music wing'd instead of silent plumes
To hover round my head, and make me sick
Of joy and grief at once. Grief overcame,
And I was stopping up my frantic ears,
When, past all hindrance of my trembling hands,
A voice came sweeter, sweeter than all tune,
And still it cried, 'Apollo! young Apollo!
The morning-bright Apollo! young Apollo!'
I fled, it follow'd me, and cried, 'Apollo!' "

Beauty is also a revelation to the gods themselves in their own bosoms where it has sprung into life. The passage in which Apollo's awakening is described — full of a poet's personal touches of his own experience in coming into possession of himself — is one of the most impassioned in all Keats's writing:

" Together had he left his mother fair
And his twin-sister sleeping in their bower,
And in the morning twilight wandered forth
Beside the osiers of a rivulet,
Full ankle-deep in lilies of the vale.
The nightingale had ceased, and a few stars
Were lingering in the heavens, while the thrush
Began calm-throated. Throughout all the isle
There was no covert, no retired cave
Unhaunted by the murmurous noise of waves,
Though scarcely heard in many a green recess.
He listen'd, and he wept, and his bright tears
Went trickling down the golden bow he held.
Thus with half-shut suffusèd eyes he stood,
While from beneath some cumbrous boughs hard by
With solemn step an awful Goddess came,
And there was purport in her looks for him,
Which he with eager guess began to read
Perplex'd, the while melodiously he said:
'How cam'st thou over the unfooted sea?
Or hath that antique mien and robèd form
Moved in these vales invisible till now?
Sure I have heard those vestments sweeping o'er
The fallen leaves, when I have sat alone
In cool mid-forest. Surely I have traced
The rustle of those ample skirts about
These grassy solitudes, and seen the flowers
Lift up their heads, and still the whisper pass'd.
Goddess! I have beheld those eyes before,
And their eternal calm, and all that face

Or I have dream'd.' — 'Yes,' said the supreme shape,
'Thou hast dream'd of me; and awaking up
Didst find a lyre all golden by thy side,
Whose strings touch'd by thy fingers, all the vast
Unwearied ear of the whole universe
Listen'd in pain and pleasure at the birth
Of such new tuneful wonder. Is 't not strange
That thou shouldst weep, so gifted? Tell me, youth,
What sorrow thou canst feel; for I am sad
When thou dost shed a tear: explain thy griefs
To one who in this lonely isle hath been
The watcher of thy sleep and hours of life,
From the young day when first thy infant hand
Pluck'd witless the weak flowers, till thine arm
Could bend that bow heroic to all times.
Show thy heart's secret to an ancient Power
Who hath forsaken old and sacred thrones
For prophecies of thee, and for the sake
Of loveliness new-born.' — Apollo then,
With sudden scrutiny and gloomless eyes,
Thus answer'd, while his white melodious throat
Throbb'd with the syllables: — 'Mnemosyne!
Thy name is on my tongue, I know not how;
Why should I tell thee what thou so well seest?
Why should I strive to show what from thy lips
Would come no mystery? For me, dark, dark,
And painful vile oblivion seals my eyes:
I strive to search wherefore I am so sad,
Until a melancholy numbs my limbs;
And then upon the grass I sit, and moan,

Like one who once had wings. — O why should I
Feel cursed and thwarted, when the liegeless air
Yields to my step aspirant? why should I
Spurn the green turf as hateful to my feet?
Goddess benign, point forth some unknown thing:
Are there not other regions than this isle?
What are the stars? There is the sun, the sun!
And the most patient brilliance of the moon!
And stars by thousands! Point me out the way
To any one particular beauteous star,
And I will flit into it with my lyre,
And make its silvery splendour pant with bliss
I have heard the cloudy thunder: Where is power?
Whose hand, whose essence, what divinity
Makes this alarum in the elements,
While I here idle listen on the shores
In fearless yet in aching ignorance?
O tell me, lonely Goddess, by thy harp,
That waileth every morn and eventide,
Tell me why thus I rave, about these groves!
Mute thou remainest. — Mute! yet I can read
A wondrous lesson in thy silent face:
Knowledge enormous makes a God of me.
Names, deeds, grey legends, dire events, rebellious,
Majesties, sovran voices, agonies,
Creations and destroyings, all at once
Pour into the wide hollows of my brain,
And deify me, as if some blithe wine
Or bright elixir peerless I had drunk,
And so become immortal.' — Thus the God,

While his enkindled eyes, with level glance
Beneath his white soft temples, steadfast kept
Trembling with light upon Mnemosyne.
Soon wild commotions shook him, and made flush
All the immortal fairness of his limbs:
Most like the struggle at the gate of death;
Or liker still to one who should take leave
Of pale immortal death, and with a pang
As hot as death 's is chill, with fierce convulse
Die into life: so young Apollo anguish'd:
His very hair, his golden tresses famed
Kept undulation round his eager neck.
During the pain Mnemosyne upheld
Her arms as one who prophesied. — At length
Apollo shriek'd; — and lo! from all his limbs
Celestial. . . ."

The birth-cry of Apollo was the death-cry of Keats: there the golden pen fell from his hands, and the poem — a fragment — ends.

There is one detail in Keats's work, which though it is subsidiary, deserves mention because it completes the reality of the Titan Myth in an important way. In all the other writers, whom I have named, you do not get any idea of the Titans physically, you do not see them as Titans. In Shelley, and the rest, Prometheus is essentially a man; he has human proportion; in Keats Prometheus does not appear at all. But Keats has realized the Titanic figures to the imagination as distinct and noble forms; they have the massiveness of limb and immobility of feature that we associate with Egyptian art, with the Sphinxes and the Memnons; yet each is characterized differently; Saturn, Oceanus, Enceladus, Thea, Mnemosyne are individualized, and especially Hyperion is set forth, in ways of grandeur. The subject would require more illustration than I can now give it; but let me cite the very remarkable figure which is found in the second version of "Hyperion," a version that is as full of Dante as the first one is of Milton. The figure is that of Moneta, the solitary and ageless priestess of the temple of the Titans, "sole goddess of its desolation," who gives the poet the vision of the past.

"*And yet I had a terror of her robes,*
And chiefly of the veils that from her brow
Hung pale, and curtain'd her in mysteries,
That made my heart too small to hold its blood.
This saw that Goddess, and with sacred hand
Parted the veils. Then saw I a wan face,
Not pin'd by human sorrows, but bright-blanch'd
By an immortal sickness which kills not;
It works a constant change, which happy death
Can put no end to; deathwards progressing
To no death was that visage; it had past
The lily and the snow; and beyond these
I must not think now, though I saw that face.
But for her eyes I should have fled away;

They held me back with a benignant light,
Soft, mitigated by divinest lids
Half-clos'd, and visionless entire they seem'd
Of all external things; they saw me not,
But in blank splendour beam'd, like the mild moon,
Who comforts those she sees not, who knows not
What eyes are upward cast."

A similar imaginative power to that shown here pervades Keats's conceptions of the Titans, and distinguishes his work from all others as a creation in the visible world of the imagination such as is not elsewhere to be found. Here only is the Titan world made nobly real.

I fear to weary you with this long catalogue of the various modern forms of the Titan Myth, but it is necessary to develop the theme. I must say at least a word about Goethe's "Prometheus." It is only a brief fragment of a drama, and belongs to his youth. He was but twenty-four when he experimented with it. In the scenes which we possess, Prometheus is the maker of the clay images to which he gives life by the aid of Pallas — that is, really, by his own intelligence. He launches them as men in the career of civilization by declaring to them the principle of property; he tells one to build a house, and to the question whether it will be for the man himself or for everybody, Prometheus answers it shall be the man's own private possession and dwelling; he declares also the principle of retaliatory justice, saying on the occasion of the first theft, that he whose hand is against every one, every one's hand shall be against him; and he announces the fact and meaning of the first death. The drama does not proceed further. Its significance lies in two points; in the first place it is easy to see in Prometheus's attitude toward his clay images and his language about them a reflection of the young poet's own state of mind toward the mental beings whom he creates — a reflection, that is, of the pride and glory of genius in imaginary creation. Secondly, and more importantly, the drama exhibits the intense desire of the young Goethe for complete individual independence. In the answer Prometheus makes to the messenger of Zeus, who remonstrates with him, the central point is that Prometheus feels he is a god like Zeus, and wants freedom to do his will in his own realm as Zeus does in Olympus. Let Zeus keep his own, and let me keep my own, he says; he would rather his clay images should never live than be subjects of Zeus, for being still unborn, they are still free; liberty is the true good, and men, made by him, shall be embodiments of his own independent spirit. In all this is the prophecy of Goethe's own life. To me Goethe is the type of the man who wants to be let alone; and he accomplished his desire in a supremely selfish tranquillity, in which he used life to develop himself, sacrificed all things to himself, was at once the model and the condemnation of self-culture so pursued. In his young Prometheus there is this impatient cry for individual liberty, as a basis of life; and I discern little else significant in it. I must also spare a word for Victor Hugo's "Titan." The poem is in the "Legend of the Ages." This Titan is not Prometheus, or any other individual Titan, but is all of them in one, the giant, conceived as *one.* He is, of course, mankind — earth-born man, conceived as in scientific history, burrowing his way out of the planet itself — a massive mediæval creature, gross and violent, tearing his path through cave and grotto, till at last he emerges and sees the stars. This giant is clearly a symbol of man rising from his crude earthliness of nature and barbaric ages up to the sight and knowledge of the heavenly world. It is a type of progress, as science and history jointly conceive the evolution of humanity.

I have sufficiently illustrated how the Titan Myth in its variety has been employed to embody and express the idea of a progressive humanity in many aspects as it has appeared to different poets. The idea of progress is in our civilization a continuing and universal idea; and Prometheus is a continuing and universal image of its nature — the race-image of a race-idea. The Promethean situation is inherent in the law of human progress, however viewed, whether historically or scientifically or ethically, or in any other way. Emerson says

> "*The fiend that man harries,*
> *Is Love of the Best.*"

The dream of this Best, and the will to bring it down to earth — the struggle with the temporary ruling worse that is in the world and must be dethroned — the proud and resolute suffering of all that such a present world can inflict — the faith in the final victory, are the Promethean characteristics; but the human spirit, in the nature of the case, must forever be in bonds; its successive liberations are partial only, and in the disclosure of a forever fairer dream in the future, lies also the disclosure of new bonds, for the present is always a state of chains in view of the to-morrow; and for man there is always to-morrow. The great words that seem the keys of progress, such as reason, love, beauty, are only symbols of an infinite series in life — a series that never ends. Such is the abstract statement that progress involves the idea of humanity as a Promethean sufferer. But the race, which requires picturesque and vivid images of its highest faith, hope and thought, comes to its poets, like the human child, and says ever and ever — "Tell me a story: tell me a story about myself." And the poet tells the race a new story about itself — like the mother of Marius when she told him of "the white bird which he must bear in his bosom across the crowded market-place — his soul." Each poet tells this new story to the child about itself — a story it did not know before, and the child believes the story and increases knowledge and life with it. The question the race asks, in this Myth, is "what is most divine in me?" "What is the god in me?" — and Shelley answers, it is all-enduring and all-forgiving love toward all; and Herder answers that it is reason, Keats that it is beauty, Goethe that it is liberty, and Hugo that it is immense triumphant toil; and each in giving his answer tells the story of the old gods and the younger gods, and the wise Titan who knew yet other gods that should come. And the race listens to these tales because it hears in them its own voice speaking. Men of genius are men, like other men; but their genius, if I may use an obvious comparison, is like the reflector in front of the light-house flame — in all directions but one it is a common flame, but in that one direction along which the reflector magnifies, glorifies and speeds its radiance, it is the shining of a great light. Look at men of genius, as you find them in biography, and they seem ordinary persons of daily affairs; but if you can catch sight of genius through that side which is turned out to the infinite as to a great ocean, you will see, I will not say the man himself, but the use God makes of the man.

That use is to reveal ourselves to ourselves, to show what human nature is and can do, to unlock our minds, our hearts, all our energies, for use. We admire and love such men because they are more ourselves than we are, the undeveloped, often unknown selves that in us are but partially born. "What is most divine in me?" is the question the race puts; and perhaps it is true (though the statement may be startling), that as soon as man discovers a god in himself, all external gods fall from their thrones — and this is the meaning of the myth. But again, what is this but the old verse —

"*The kingdom of heaven is within you?*"

That realized, the old gods may go their ways. It is realized, perhaps, for one of its modes, in this way: that as the being of beauty is entire and perfect in the grass that flourishes for a summer, or in the rose of dawn that fades even while it blossoms, so the power of moral ideas enters, entire and perfect, into our being, and, as I said, the humblest of men suffering for man's good as he conceives it shares in the moral sublimity of Prometheus. What is thus within man — the thing that is most divine — is certainly the medium by which man approaches the divinity, and through which he beholds it, in any living way. It belongs to Puritanism, as a mood of mind, to be impatient of any external thing between the soul and the divinity; it will have the least of any such material element in its spiritual sight and communion; it sees god by an inner vision. Mediums of some sort there must be between human nature and its idea of the divine; and it seems to me that our inner vision by which the Puritan spirit reaches outward and upward is the vision of imagination transfiguring history to saints and martyrs in their holy living and holy dying, transfiguring all human experience to the idealities of poetry. Mankind seeing itself more perfect in St. Francis, in Philip Sidney, in all men of spiritual genius, makes them a part of this inner vision — and, rank over rank, above them the perfection of Arthur and Parsifal, and still more high the perfection of reason, beauty, and love in their element. In this hierarchy of human daring, dreaming, desiring is the only beatific vision that human eyes ever immediately beheld — the vision of what is most divine in man. What I maintain is that, humanly speaking, in the search for God one path by which the race moves on is through this inner vision of ideal perfections in its own nature and its own experience, which it has fixed and illuminated in these imaginative figures, these race-images of race-ideas.

The Torch

V

SPENSER

The general principle which I have endeavoured to set forth in the first four lectures is that mankind in the process of civilization stores up race-power, in one or another form, so that it is a continually growing fund; and that literature, pre-eminently, is such a store of spiritual race-power, derived originally from the historical life or from the general experience of men, and transformed by imagination so that all which is not necessary falls away from it and what is left is truth in its simplest, most vivid and vital form. Thus I instanced mythology, chivalry, and the Scriptures as three such sifted deposits of the past; and I illustrated the use poetry makes of such race-images and race-ideas by the example of the myth of the Titans. In the remaining four lectures I desire to approach the same general principle of the storing of race-power from the starting-point of the individual author — to set forth Spenser, Milton, Wordsworth and Shelley, not in their personality but as race-exponents, and to show that their essential greatness and value are due to the degree in which they availed themselves of the race-store. You may remember that I defined education for all men as the process of identifying oneself with the race-mind, entering into and taking possession of the race-store; and the rule is the same for men of genius as for other men. You find, consequently, that the greatest poets have always been the best scholars of their times — not in the encyclopædic sense that they knew everything, but in the sense that they possessed the living knowledge of their age, so far as it concerns the human soul and its history. They have always possessed what is called the academic mind — that is, they had a strong grasp on literary tradition and the great thoughts of mankind, and the great forms which those thoughts had taken on in the historic imagination. Virgil is a striking example of such a poet, perfectly cultivated in all the artistic, philosophic, literary tradition as it then was: Dante and Chaucer are similar instances; and, in English, Spenser, Milton, Gray, Shelley and Tennyson continue the line of those poets in whom scholarship — the academic tradition — is an essential element in their worth. It ought not to be necessary to bring this out so clearly; for it is obvious that men of genius, in the process of absorbing the race-store, by the very fact become scholarly men, men of intellectual culture, though in consequence of their genius they neglect all culture except that which still has spiritual life in it. This is so elementary a truth in literature that the index to the importance of an author is often his representative power — the degree to which he sums up and delivers the human past. How large a tract of time, what extent of knowledge, what range of historical emotion — does his mind drain? These are initial questions. And in literary history, you know, there are here and there minds, so central to the period, such meeting points of different ages and cultures, that they resemble those junctions on a railway map which seem to absorb all geography into their own black dots. The greatest poets are just such centres of spiritual history; where ancient and modern meet, where classicism and mediævalism, Christianity and paganism, Renaissance and Reformation and Revolution *meet* — there is the focus, for the time being, of the soul of man; and it is at that point that genius developes its transcendent power.

Spenser was such a mind. I spoke in the first lecture of that law of progress which involves the passing away of a civilization at the moment of its perfection and the death of that breed of men who have brought it to its height. Spenser was the poet of a dying race and a dying culture; in his work there is reflected and embodied a climax in the spiritual life of humanity to which imagination gives form, beauty, and passion. In this respect I am always reminded of Virgil when I read him; for Virgil used, like Spenser, the romanticism of a receding past to express his sense of human life, and he was related to his materials in much the same way. The Myth of Arthur lay behind Spenser as the Myth of Troy lay behind Virgil in the mist of his country's origins; the Italians of the Renaissance, Ariosto, and Tasso, were a school for Spenser much as the Alexandrian poets had been for Virgil; and as in Virgil mythology and Homeric heroism and the legend of the antique Italian land before Rome blended in one, and became the last flowering of the pre-Christian world in what is, perhaps, the greatest of all world-poems, the "Æneid," so in Spenser chivalry, mediævalism and the new birth of learning in Europe blended, and gave us a world-poem of the Christian soul, in which mediæval spirituality — as it seems to me — expired. Spenser resembled Virgil, too, in his moment; he was endeavouring to create for England a poem such as Italy possessed in Ariosto's and Tasso's epics, to introduce into his country's literature the most supreme poetic art then in the world, just as Virgil was attempting to instil into the Roman genius the imaginative art of Greece. He resembled Virgil again in his poetic education inasmuch as he formed his powers and first exercised them in pastoral verse, in the "Shephard's Kalendar" as Virgil did in his "Eclogues"; and he resembled Virgil still more importantly in that his theme was the greatest known to him — namely, the empire of the soul, as Virgil's was the empire of Rome. Spenser, then, when he came to his work is to be looked on as a master of all literary learning, a pioneer and planter of poetic art in his own country, and a poet who used the world of the receding past as his means of expressing what was most real to him in human life.

The work by which he is remembered is "The Færie Queene," and in it all that I have said meets you at the threshold. Perhaps the first, and certainly the abiding impression the poem makes, is of its remoteness from life. Remoteness, you know, is said to be a necessary element in any artistic effect — such as you feel in looking at Greek statues or Italian Madonnas or French landscapes. This remoteness of the artistic world the poem has, in large measure: its country is no physical region known to geography, but is that land of the plain where Knights are always pricking, of forests and streams and hills that have no element of composition, and especially of a horizon like the sea's, usually lonely, but where anything may appear at any time: it is a land like a dream; and what takes place there at any moment is pictorial, and can be painted. But the quality of remoteness, so noticeable in the poem and to which I refer, is not that of artistic atmosphere and setting. It arises largely from the remoteness of history in the poem, felt in the constant presence of outworn things, of bygone characters, ways and incidents; and the impression of intricacy that the poem also makes at first, the sense of confusion in it, is partly due to this same presence of the unfamiliar in most heterogeneous variety. This miscellaneousness is the result of Spenser's comprehensive inclusion in the poem of all he knew, that is, of the entire literary tradition of the race within his ken. Thus you find, at the outset, Aristotle's scheme of the moral virtues, and Plato's doctrine of the unity of beauty and wisdom, on the philosophical side; and for imagery out of the classics, here are Plato, Proserpina, and Night, the house of Morpheus, the bleeding tree, the cloud that envelopes the fallen warrior and allows him to escape, the journey in Hades, the story of "Hippolytus," and fauns, satyrs and other minor mythological beings. You find, also, out of mediæval things, the method of the poem which is the characteristic mediæval method of allegory, and in imagery dragons, giants, dwarfs, the hermit, the magician, the dungeon, the wood of error, the dream of Arthur, the holy wells, the Saracen Knights, the House of Pride, the House of Holiness, and many more; and, in these lists, I have cited instances only from the first of the six books. A similar rich variety of matter is to be found, consisting of the characteristic belongings of Renaissance fable. This multiplicity of imaginative detail, being as it is a summary of all the poetical knowledge of previous time, is perplexing to a reader unfamiliar with the literature before Spenser, and makes the poem seem really, and not merely artistically remote. Here appears most clearly the fact which I emphasize, that the "Færie Queene" depicts and contains a receding world, a dying culture; for it is to be borne in mind that to Spenser and his early readers these things were not then so remote; mediævalism was as near to him as Puritanism is to us, and the thoughts, methods, aims, language and imagery of the Renaissance as near as the Revolution is to us. In that age, too, chivalry yet lingered, at least as a spectacle, and other materials in the poem that now seem to us like stage-machinery were part and parcel of real life. The tourney was still a game of splendid pleasure and display at the Court of Elizabeth; the masque-procession, so constant in one or another form in the poem, was a fashion of Christmas mummery, of the Court Masque, and of city processions; the physical aspect and furniture of the poem were, thus, not wholly antiquated; and on the side of character, it is easy to read between the lines the presence of Spenser's own noble friends — and no one in that age was richer in noble friendship — the presence, I mean, of the just Lord Grey, the adventurous Raleigh, and the high-spirited Philip Sidney. The element of historical remoteness must, therefore, be thought of as originally much less strong than now, and one which the passage of time has imported into the poem very largely.

We are, perhaps, too apt to think that our own age is one in which great heterogeneousness of knowledge, of thought and principle and faith, is a distinctive trait; but we are not the first to find our race-inheritance a confusion of riches, and a tentative electicism the best we can compass in getting a philosophy of our own. Every learned and open mind, in the times of the flowing together of the world's ideas, has the same experience. Spenser, being a receptive mind and standing at the centre of the ideas of the world then, was necessarily overwhelmed with the variety of his knowledge; but he faced the same problem that Milton, Gray, Shelley, and Tennyson in their time met; the problem of how to reduce this miscellaneousness of matter to some order, to reconcile it with his own mind, to build up out of it his own world. It is the same problem that confronts each one of us, in education; in the presence of this race-inheritance, so vast, so apparently contradictory and diverse — how to take possession of it, to make it ours vitally, to have it enter into and take possession of us. Spenser is an admirable example of this situation, for in his poem the opposition between the race-mind and the individual is clearly brought out in the point that he converges all this imagery, knowledge and method in order to set forth the individual's life. Spenser states his purpose in the preface: "The general end," he says, "of all the Book is to fashion a gentleman, or noble person, in vertuous and gentle discipline." It is the very problem before each of us in education: "to fashion a gentleman." Spenser's plan, in portraying how this is to be done, is a very simple one. By a gentleman he means a man of Christian virtue, perfected in all the graces and the powers of human nature. The education required is an education in the development of the virtues, as he named them — Holiness, Temperance, Chastity, Friendship, Justice, Courtesy; he illustrates the development of each virtue, one in each Knight, and sends each Knight forth on an adventure in the course of which the Knight meets and overcomes the characteristic temptations of the virtue which he embodies. This was the plan of the poem, which, however, the poet found it easier to formulate than to follow with precision. The main fact stands out, however, that Spenser used all his resources of knowledge and art, miscellaneous as they were, for the single purpose of showing how the soul comes to moral perfection in the Christian world. You see there is nothing contemporary or remote or by-gone in the problem: that is universal and unchanging; but in answering it Spenser used an imaginative language that to many of us is like a lost tongue. Shall we, then, let the allegory go, as Lowell advised, content that it does not bite us, as he says? I cannot bring myself to second that advice. Though I am as fond of the idols of poetry for their own sake as any one, yet I have room for idols of morality and philosophy also — let us have as many idols as we can get, is my way: and to leave out of our serious-minded Spenser what was to the poet himself the core of his meaning — its spirituality — is too violent a measure, and bespeaks such desperate dullness in the allegory as I do not find in it. To read the poem for the beauty of its surface, and to let the noble substance go, is, at all events, not the way to understand it as a focus of race-elements and a store of race-power, as a poem not of momentary delight, but of historical phases of knowledge, culture and aspiration, a poem of the thoughtful human spirit brooding over its long inheritance of beauty, honour, and virtue.

Of course, I cannot in an hour convey much of an idea of so great a poem, so various in its loveliness, so profound in significance, so diversified in merely literary interest. I shall make no attempt to tell its picturesque and wandering story, to describe its characters, or to explain what marvellous lives they led in that old world of romance. But I shall try to show, in general terms, certain aspects of it as a poem that presents life in a universal, vital, and never-to-be-antiquated way, such as it seemed to one of the most noble-natured of Englishmen, in a great age of human effort, thought and accomplishment.

Among the primary images under which life has been figured, none is more universal and constant than that into which the idea of travel enters. To all men at all times life has been a voyage, a pilgrimage, a quest. Spenser conceived of it as the quest, the peculiar image of chivalry, but not as the quest for the Grail or any other shadowy symbol on the attainment of which the quest was ended in a mystic solution. The quest of his Knights is for self-mastery; and it is achieved at each forward step of the journey. You remember that in the lecture on Prometheus I illustrated the way in which man takes a certain part of his nature — the evil principle — and places it outside of himself, calls it Mephistopheles, and so deals with it artistically; in Spenser, the temptation which each Knight is under is his worser self, as we say, so taken and placed outside as his enemy whom he overcomes; thus, Guyon, the Knight of temperance, overcomes the various forms of anger, of avarice, and of voluptuousness, which are merely, in fact, his other and worser selves; in each victory he gathers strength for the next encounter, and so ends perfecting himself in that virtue. Life — that is to say, the quest — has a goal in self-mastery, that is progressively reached by the Knight at each new stage of his struggle. The atmosphere of life — so conceived as a spiritual warfare — is broadly rendered; it is, for example, always a thing of danger, and this element is given through the changing incident, the deceits practised on the Knights, the troubles they fall into, often unwittingly, and undeservedly, their constant need to be vigilant and to receive succor. The secret, the false, the insidious, are as often present as is the warfare of the open foe. Again, this life is a thing of mystery. However clear we may try to make life, however positive in mind we are and armed against illusions, it still remains true that mystery envelopes life. I do not mean the mystery of thought, of the unknown, but the mystery of life itself. Spenser conceives this mystery as the action, friendly or inimical, of a spiritual world round about man, a supernatural world; and he renders it by means of enchantment. I dare say that to most readers the presence of enchantment, both evil and good, is a hindrance to the appreciation of the poem and impairs its reality to their minds. Arthur, you know, has a veiled shield; but its bared radiance will overthrow of itself any foe. This seems like an unfair advantage, and takes interest from the poem. Such enchanted weapons may be regarded as symbolic of the higher nature of the cause in which they are employed, of its inward power, and possibly of the true powers of the heroes, their spiritual force, and it may be that this emphasis on the spirituality of their force is the true reason for the introduction of the symbol; for these are not only Knights human, but Knights Christian and clothed with a might which is not of this world. Such an explanation, though plausible, seems mechanical; the truth which it contains is that the enchanted arms do not denote a higher degree of physical strength, as if the Knights had rifles instead of spears, but a difference of spiritual power. It is, however, much more clear that by the realm of enchantment in the poem is figured the interest which the supernatural world takes in man's conflict — the mediæval idea that God and his angels are on one side and the devil and his angels are on the other; and the presence of enchantment in the poem is a means of expressing this belief. The reality of divine aid against devilish machination is thus symbolized; but in one particular this aid is so important a matter that Spenser introduces it in a more essential and, in fact, in a human way. To Spenser's mind, no man could save himself, or perfect himself in virtue even, without Divine Grace; this was the doctrine he held, and, therefore, he made Arthur the special representative and instrument of Grace, and at each point of the story where the Knight cannot retrieve himself from the danger into which he had fallen, Arthur appears with his glorious arms for the rescue. The presence of mystery in life, too, is not only thus felt in the atmosphere of enchantment and in the signal acts of rescue by Arthur, but it also envelopes the cardinal abstract ideas of the poem — such ideas, I mean, as wisdom in Una, and as chastity in Britomart, to whose beauty (which is of course, the imaging forth of the special virtue of each) is ascribed a miraculous power of mastery, as in Una's case over the Lion and the foresters, and in Britomart's case over Artegal.

> " *And he himselfe long gazing there upon,*
> *At last fell humbly downe upon his knee,*
> *And of his wonder made religion,*
> *Weening some heavenly goddesse he did see.*"

This is that radiance which Plato first saw in the countenance of Truth, such that, he said, were Truth to come among men unveiled in her own form, all men would worship her. So Spenser, learning from Plato, presents the essential loveliness of all virtue as having inherent power to overcome — precisely, you will remember, as

Keats describes the principle of beauty in "Hyperion" as inherently victorious.

The idea of life as a quest, with an atmosphere of danger and mystery, and presided over by great principles such as wisdom, grace, chastity, so clad in loveliness to the moral sense that they seem like secondary forms of Divine being — these are fundamental conceptions in the poem, its roots, so to speak, and they belong in the ethical sphere. But Spenser was the most poetically minded of all English poets; he not only knew that however true and exalted his ideas of life might be, they must come forth from his mind as images, but he also by nature loved truth in the image more than in the abstract; and he therefore approached truth through the imagination rather than through the intellect. That is to say, he was a poet, first and foremost; and wove his poem of sensuous effects. Sensibility to all things of sense was his primary endowment; he was a lover of beauty, of joy, and his joy in beauty reached such a pitch that he excels all English poets in a certain artistic voluptuousness of nature, which was less rich in Milton and less pure in Keats, who alone are to be compared with him, as poets of sensuous endowment. It is seldom that the artistic nature appears in the English race; it belongs rather to the southern peoples, and especially to Italy; but when it does arise in the English genius, and blends happily there with the high moral spirit which is a more constant English trait — especially when it blends with the Puritan strain, it seems as if the young Plato had been born again. Both Milton and Spenser were Puritans who were lovers of beauty; and Spenser showed Milton that way of grace. No language can exaggerate the extent to which Spenser was permeated with this sensuousness of temperament, and he created the body of his poem out of it — the colour, the picture, the incident, figures and places, the atmosphere, the cadence and the melody of it. You feel this bodily delight in the very fall of the lines, interlacing and sinuous, with Italian softness, smoothness, and slide. You feel it in his love of gardens and streams; in his love of pictured walls, and all the characteristic adornments of Renaissance art; in his grouping of human figures in the various forms of the masque; in his descriptions of wealth and luxury, of the bower of bliss, of the scenes of mythology; in every part of the poem the flowing of this fount of beauty is the one unfailing thing. It came to him from the Italian Renaissance, of course. It is the Renaissance element in the poem; and with it all the other elements are suffused.

The worship of beauty, as it was known in all objects of art, and in all poetry which had formed itself, in description and motive, on objects of art, was perhaps its centre; but, in Spenser, it exceeded such bounds, and, though taken from the Renaissance, it was given a new career in Puritanism. For the singular thing about this sensuous sensibility in Spenser, this artistic voluptuousness in the sight and presence of beauty, is that it remained pure in spirit. In Renaissance poetry, using the same chivalric tradition as Spenser, this spirit has ended in Ariosto's "Orlando" — a poem of cynicism, as it seems to me. It is to the honour of the moral genius of the English that the Renaissance spirit in poetry, in their tongue, issued in so nobly different a poem as "The Færie Queene." This was because, as I say, the Renaissance worship of beauty was given a new career by Spenser in Puritanism. Perhaps I can best illustrate the matter by bringing forward what was one of Spenser's noblest points. He raised this worship of beauty to the highest point of ideality by having recourse to the tradition of chivalry in its worship of woman, and blended the two in a new worship of womanhood. I think it will be agreed that, although Spenser's romance is primarily one of the adventures of men, it is his female characters that live most vividly in the memory of the reader. These characters are, indeed, very simple and elementary ones; they are not elaborated on the scale to which the novel has accustomed our minds; but they are of the same kind, it seems to me, as Shakspere's equally simple types of womanhood — such as Cordelia, Imogen, Miranda — of which they were prophetic. What I desire to bring out, however, is not their simplicity, but the fact that they enter the poem to ennoble it, to raise it in spiritual power, and to strengthen the heroes in their struggles. In this respect, as I think, Spenser did a new thing. In the epic, generally, woman comes on the scene only to impair the moral quality and the manly actions of the hero: such was Dido, you remember, in the "Æneid," and Eve in "Paradise Lost," and the same story, with slight qualifications holds of other epic poems. It is a high distinction that in Spenser womanhood is presented, not as the source of evil, its presence and its temptation, but as the inspiration to life for such Knights as Artegal, the Red-Cross Knight, and others; and, furthermore, the worship of beauty, which they found in the worship of womanhood, is in Spenser hardly to be distinguished from the worship of those principles, which I have described as secondary forms of Divine being — the principles of wisdom, chastity and the like. I find in these idealities of womanhood the highest reach of the poem, and in them blend harmoniously the chivalric, artistic and moral elements of Spenser's mind. And as we feel in Spenser's men the near presence of such friends as Lord Grey, Raleigh and Sidney, it is not fanciful to feel here the neighbourhood of Elizabethan women — such as she of whom Jonson wrote the great epitaph:

"*Underneath this sable hearse*
Lies the subject of all verse;
Sidney's sister, Pembroke's mother.
Death, ere thou hast slain another
Learned and fair and good as she,
Time shall throw a dart at thee."

With this supreme presence of womanhood in "The Færie Queene" goes the fact that warfare as such is a disappearing element; it is less prominent, and it interests less, than might be expected. This is because, just as beauty in all its forms is spiritualized in the poem, so is war; the war here described is the inner warfare of the soul with itself; it is all a symbol of spiritual struggle, and necessarily it seems less real as a thing of outward event. The poem is one of thought, essentially; its action has to be interpreted in terms of thought before it is understood; it is, in truth, a contemplative poem, and its mood is as often the artistic contemplation of beauty, as the ethical contemplation of action. These are the two poles on which the poem moves. Yet they are opposed only in the analysis, and to our eyes; in Spenser's poem, and in his heart they were closely united, for virtue was to him the utmost of beauty, and its attainment was by the worship of beauty; so near, by certain aptitudes of emotion towards the supreme good, did he come to Plato, his teacher, and is therefore to be fitly described, in this regard, as the disciple of Plato.

I wonder whether, as I have been speaking, the poem and its author grow more or less remote to you. Spenser — this philosophical Platonist, this Renaissance artist, this Puritan moralist — does he seem more or less credible? Was it not a strange thing that he should think that the abstract development of a Christian soul, however picturesquely presented, was an important theme of poetry? Yet it is true, that the most purely poetical of English poets, and one of the most cultivated minds of Europe in his time, had this idea; and in Elizabeth's reign — that is, in a period of worldly and masculine activity, of immense vigour, in the very dawn and sunburst of an England to which our American imperial dream is but a toy of fancy — in that Elizabethan, that Shaksperian age, Spenser chose as the theme of highest moment the formation of a Christian character. I have spoken of the artistic remoteness of his poem, and of the remoteness of his literary tradition, its classical, mediæval and Renaissance matter and method; but there is a third remoteness by which it seems yet more distant — the remoteness of its spirituality. In the days about and before Spenser there was great interest in the question of character in the upper classes; what were the qualities of a courtier was debated over and over in every civilized country, and the books written about it are still famous books and worth reading. Spenser took this Renaissance idea — what is the pattern of manhood? — and — just as in the case of the worship of beauty — gave it a career in Puritanism. The question became — what is a Christian soul, perfected in human experience? What are its aims, its means, its natural history? What is its ideal life in this world of beauty, honour, service? And this question he debated in the six books of his half-completed poem, which has made him known ever since as the poet's poet. The Knight of the "Færie Queene" is the Renaissance courtier Christianized — that is all. Here is the final spiritualization of the long result of chivalry as an ideal of manly life. That is the curious thing — that the result is, not merely moral, but spiritual.

The spiritual life, in this sense, is far removed from our literature; it is so, because it is far removed from the general thought of men. The struggle men now think of as universal and typical of life, is not the clashing of spear and shield on any field of tourney, nor the fencing of the soul with any supernatural foe, seeking its damnation: it is the mere struggle for existence, with the survival of the fittest as the result: a scientific idea, and one that centres attention on the things of this world. This increases the sense in mankind of the materialism of human life and the importance of its mortal interests. Commerce seconds science in defining this struggle as a competition of trade, a conflict, on the larger scale, of tariff wars, a race for special privilege and open opportunity in new countries. Science and trade are almost as large a part of life now as righteousness was in Matthew Arnold's day: he reckoned it, I believe, at three-quarters. The result is that mankind is surrounded with a different scheme of thought, meditation and effort from that of Spenser's age. He was near the ages, that we call the ages of faith: he was not far from the old Catholic idea of discipline; he was not enfranchised from supernaturalism in Reformation dogmas; he lived when men still died for their religion; — all of which is to say that the idea of the spiritual in man's life and its importance, was nigh and close to him. In our literature there is much presentation of moral character, in the sense of the side that a man turns toward his fellow beings in society: in Scott, Thackeray and in Dickens, George Eliot — to name the greatest, this is found; but such spiritual character as Spenser made the subject of his meditation and picturing is not found. In the history of literature, the hero of action has always ended by developing into the saintly ideal: so it was in Paganism from Achilles to Æneas; so it was in mediævalism from Roland and Lancelot to Arthur, Galahad and Parsifal;

and in this chivalric tradition Spenser is the last term. Will our moral ideal, as it is now flourishing, show a similar course — has our literature of the democratic movement, now in its early stages, the making of such a saint in it — that is, of the man to whom God only is real? — as Paganism and mediævalism in their day evolved?

Spenser, then, being so remote from us, in all ways — the question is natural, why read his poem at all? Because it is the flower of long ages: because you command in it as in a panorama the poetical tradition of all the great imaginative literature in previous centuries, classical, mediæval and Renaissance; because you see how Spenser, by his appropriation of these elements became himself the Platonist, the artist, the moralist, and fused all in the passion for beauty on earth and in the heavens above, and so centred his whole nature toward God; and what took place in him may take place, according to its measure, in us. For, though the thoughts of men change from century to century, and one guiding principle yields to another, and the ideal life is built up in new ways in successive generations, yet the soul's life remains, however cast in new forms of the old passion for beauty and virtue. If Spenser be a poet's poet, as they say, let him appeal to the poet in you — for in every man there is a poet; let him appeal in his own way, as a teacher of the spiritual life; and, if my wish might prevail, let him come most home to you and receive intimate welcome as the Puritan lover of beauty.

The Torch

VI

MILTON

Milton is a great figure in our minds. He is a very lonely figure. For one thing, he has no companions of genius round him; there is no group about him, in his age. Again, he was a blind old man, and there is something in blindness that, more than anything else, isolates a man; and in his case, by strange but powerful contrast, his blindness is enlarged and glorified by the fact that he saw all the glory of the angels and the Godhead as no other mortal eye ever beheld them, and the fact that he was blind makes the vision itself more credible. And thirdly he has impressed himself on men's memories as unique in character; and, in his age defeated and given o'er, among his enemies exposed and left, with the Puritan cause lost, he is the very type and pattern of a great spirit in defeat — imprisoned in his blindness, poor, neglected, yet still faithful and the master of his own integrity; for us, almost as much as a poet, he remains the intellectual champion of human liberty. So through centuries there has slowly formed itself this lonely figure in our minds as our thought of Milton, and as Cæsar is a universal name of imperial power, the name of Milton has become a synonym of moral majesty. But it was not thus that he was thought of in his own times. There is no evidence that Cromwell or the other important men of the state knew that Milton was greater than they, or that he was truly great at all; to them he was pre-eminently a secretary in the state department. The next generation of poets—Dryden—called him "the old schoolmaster," you remember. In his earlier years he appealed to the taste of a few cultivated and travelled gentlemen, like Sir Henry Wotton, as a graceful and noble-languaged poet; but it was a full generation after his death that he was accepted into the roll of the great, by Addison in the "Spectator," and the next century was well on its way before he was imitated by new men as the English model of blank verse. In the literary tradition of England, however, he is now established, and for all of us he stands apart, a majestic memory, as I have said, touched with the sublimity of his subject and with the sublimity of his own character. There is, too, in our thoughts of him, something grim, something of the sterner aspect of historical Puritanism; the softness of Spenser, the softness of his youth, had gone out of him, and he had all the hardness of man in him — he was trained down to the last ounce — he was austere. Yet I love to recall his youth — you remember the fair boy-face of the first portrait — a face of singular beauty; and you know his pink and white complexion was such at the University that he was called "the Lady of Christ's"; and, in those first years of his poetizing, he was deep in the loveliest verse of Greece and Italy, in Pindar and Euripides, in Petrarch and Tasso, as well as in Shakspere and Spenser who were his English masters. He was a young humanist — filled to overflowing with the new learning and its artistic products, a lover of them and of music, and of everything beautiful in nature — he was especially a landscape-lover. Even then the clear spirit — the white soul — somewhat too unspotted for human affections to cling about, it may be — was there; you hear it singing in the high and piercing melody of the "Hymn on the Morning of Christ's Nativity," which happily is usually a child's first knowledge of him; a certain loofness of nature he has, and nowhere do you find in his English verse — nor do I find it in his Latin verse where it is sometimes thought to be — nowhere do you find the note of friendship, of that companionableness which is often so charming a trait in the young lives of the poets. But within his own reserves — and perhaps the more precious and refined for that very reason —

there was the same sensuous delight in the artistic things of sense, in natural beauty, in romantic charm, in the lines of the old poets, that there was in Spenser; and in this he was, as we mark literary descent, the child of Spenser, though of course it was fed in him from other sources and in larger measure, too. For he was a better scholar than Spenser — his times allowed him to be — and he had a far more powerful intellect. But, in these years of his milder and happier youth, when he was living in the country in his long studies — he was a student at ease till thirty — and when he was travelling in Italy, he was in the true path of Spenser and the Renaissance, the path of beauty. Thus he writes in a letter to a friend — "What besides God has resolved concerning me, I know not, but this at least: He has instilled into me at all events a vehement love of the beautiful. Not with so much labour as the fables have it, is Ceres said to have sought her daughter Proserpine, as I am wont day and night to seek for this idea of the beautiful through all the forms and faces of things (for many are the shapes of things divine) and to follow it leading me on as with certain assured traces." This is that same creed of Plato that entered so deeply into Spenser — the faith in the divine leading of beauty. How permanent its doctrine was in Milton's mind will appear later; but here its presence is to be observed, because it gives to

Milton the true quality and atmosphere of his lost youth, and also marks the great difference in tone and temper between the earlier poems — so golden phrased, so mellifluous, so happy — and the poems of his age, the "Paradise Lost" and "Regained" and the "Samson." In "Comus," more particularly in "L'Allegro" and "Il Penseroso," is the young Milton — he that the fair-haired boy grew into, the humanist student, the writer of Italian sonnets, the "landscape-lover, lord of language" — before Cromwell's age laid its heavy and manhood-enforcing hand on the poet who chose first to serve his country.

But it is the poet of whom I am to speak; and, perhaps, before entering on the subject of his verse, it may be well first to endeavour to mark his place more precisely in English poetry and to account, partially at least, for its historical distinction. A poet, so great as Milton, you may be sure, occupies some point of vantage in history; he embodies some climax in the intellectual or artistic affairs of the world; and in Milton's case there are, I think, two historical considerations not commonly brought forward. I have had a good deal to say about allegory. It was the characteristic literary form of the Middle Ages; and the substitution of the direct story of human life in its place is one of the traits of modern times. You remember that the English drama, beginning from miracle plays and moralities and passing through the stage of historical plays came finally in Shakspere to a representation of human life as it is in the most direct manner. Those of you who saw the play of "Everyman" last year have a very vivid idea of what allegory is in a drama, and how such a drama differs from "Romeo and Juliet." In "Everyman" abstract principles are personified, and their play in life illustrated; in "Romeo and Juliet," the passions and virtues are in the form of character, are humanized as we say, are there not as abstract principles but as human forces. The development of English drama from an allegorical mode of presenting life and character to a human realization of them in men and women culminated in Shakspere, who thus stood at a historic moment of climax in the evolution of his art. Now, you easily recognize the likeness of such an allegorical play as "Everyman" to Spenser's "Færie Queene," in its method of personifying the virtues and the temptations. Religious narrative poetry remained allegorical, and mediæval in artistic method, not only in Spenser, but in his successors, such as the Fletchers. Milton was the first English poet to humanize completely the characters and events of religious story, to put the religious scheme and view of the world into the form of human things, and to expel from the work the abstract allegorical element wholly. Thus he is related to previous narrative religious poetry in England precisely as Shakspere is to the moralities of early drama. He stands at this point of climax in the evolution of his particular branch of poetic art. Religious poetry was sixty years later than dramatic poetry in reaching this perfect humanization of its material; and thus it happens that Milton, though so much younger than the Elizabethans, is commonly thought of as belonging to their company and in fact the last late product of the age of their genius.

Secondly, wc are accustomed to think of the Renaissance as on the whole an affair of the southern nations, and especially of Italy; but it was a European movement, a wave of thought and peculiar passion that slowly crept up the North, and it reached its furthest point in England, and there, as I think, it reached its highest literary development. Shakspere was the climax of the Renaissance; its passion for individuality, for a free career for the human soul, and its instinct of the dignity of personal life, were the very forces to unlock most potently dramatic power; and in Shakspere this was accomplished, and you know how besides he used its material and lived in its atmosphere. Spenser, also, as I said in the last lecture, took the worship of beauty and the idea of the courtier from the Renaissance, spiritualized the one and Christianized the other, and gave them a new career in English Puritanism. Milton is to be associated with

Shakspere and Spenser, as a third and the last great representative of the Renaissance in England, and as there carrying its epic power to a degree of perfection far beyond what it had reached in Italy, exceeding both Ariosto and Tasso; in him was all the learning and taste of the Renaissance, all its cultivation of individuality and respect for it — in both matter and spirit he belonged fundamentally to that movement, and was its latest climax. I therefore define his historical position as being the point at which religious poetry was completely humanized in England, and at which the Renaissance spirit generally as a European movement culminated in epic poetry.

"Paradise Lost" is the poem by which Milton lives. Fond as we may be of his younger verse, and appreciative of the eloquence of "Paradise Regained" and of the tragic simplicity of "Samson Agonistes," yet popular judgment is to be followed in finding in "Paradise Lost" the true centre of Milton's genius. Every poet who achieves a single great poem puts his whole mind into it, empties his mind and tells all he knows; his felicity is to find a subject which permits him to do this; such was the course of Homer and Virgil, Dante, Spenser, Goethe, to name a few and Milton was no exception to the rule. He included in his poem the entire history of the universe from the heaven which was before creation to the millennium which shall be the consummation of all things; and, in this great sphere of action he chose as the objective point the moral relation of mankind to God, certainly the highest subject in importance; and in elaborating his work he used all the wealth of his literary knowledge and culture, the entire literary tradition of the race, just as Spenser did — only more broadly; whatever, either in matter or method, there was serviceable in past literature — Hebrew, Greek, Latin, Italian, and English — all this Milton used. He grasped and constructed the subject with great mental power and artistic skill; although, in minor parts, his conventional machinery and devices have been attacked, the leading lines of his construction stand clear of criticism. He really took three great themes, any one of which would have furnished forth a poem, and blended them together with such dexterity that they are seldom separated even in analysis — so perfect is the unity of the resulting whole. In the first place, you recognize at once in "Paradise Lost" a Christian adaptation of the Titan Myth. The rebellion of the angels is conceived as a war of the Titans against the gods; and is treated in accordance with Greek imagination as a conflict in which the mountains were used as weapons: —

" *From their foundations, loosening to and fro,*
They plucked the seated hills, with all their load,

Rocks, waters, woods, and by the shaggy tops
Uplifting, bore them in their hands. Amaze
Be sure, and terror, seized the rebel host
When coming towards them so dread they saw
The bottom of the mountains upward turned —
Themselves invaded next, and on their heads
Main promontories flung, which in the air
Came shadowing: — . . .
So hills amid the air encountered hills —
. . . *— horrid confusion heaped*
Upon confusion rose."

Satan on the flood of hell is conceived as of Titanic form:

" *With head uplift above the wave, and eyes*
That sparkling blazed; his other parts besides
Prone on the flood, extended long and large,
Lay floating many a rood, in bulk as huge
As whom the fables name of monstrous size,
Titanian or Earth-born, that warred on Jove,
Briareos or Typhon" —

and you recall how he reared himself from off the fiery lake, and took his station on the shore, with the ponderous shield whose "broad circumference hung on his shoulders like the moon," and stayed his steps with his tall spear —

"*To equal which the tallest pine*
Hewn on Norwegian hills, to be the mast
Of some great ammiral, were but a wand;"

and there summoning his squadrons loomed over them like the sun "in dim eclipse, disastrous twilight shedding on half the nations." Such is Satan's figure at the first, and it is by such images of Titanic darkened grandeur that his form is most vividly remembered. I have spoken of the difficulty the poets have had in defining the forms of the Titans to the eye. Milton solves the problem by ascribing to the devil and his angels no determinate form; they are, so to speak, collapsible and extensible at will; and they take the appropriate scales of proportion in whatever scene they are placed.

It is common to think of Satan as the true hero of the poem, and as an imaginative figure he certainly occupies the foreground; yet to Milton he was a hateful being, and I am convinced that familiarity with the poem takes from him that admiration which properly should belong to the hero, and at the end he is clearly felt as the object of repulsive evil, whom Milton meant him to be. Milton's method, after presenting Satan in sombre but majestic form, is gradually to debase him to the eye as well as to the mind. Here the treatment sets him apart from any conception of the Titan Prometheus in bonds; for Prometheus is never felt to be debased even physically by the punishment of Jove. The first revolt of the reader's mind from its initial admiration for Satan takes place, I think, acutely in the scene at the gate of hell when he meets Sin and Death. The association of Satan with such horrible beings as they are represented to be, and the knowledge that his intimacy with them is that of fatherhood, shocks the mind with ugliness — ugliness that is almost bestial in its effect. When he reaches the new earth, after his address to the Sun, he is seen transformed in countenance —

> " *Thus while he spake, each passion dimmed his face*
> *Thrice changed with pale — ire, envy and despair,*
> *Which marred his borrowed visage —* "

and soon he is "squat like a toad" at the ear of Eve; whence touched by the young angel's spear, he rises "the grisly King," so changed from his heavenly self that he is unrecognized. Then, after one more grand Titanic figuring of his might — the most impressive of all — as he opposes Gabriel: —

> "*On the other side, Satan, alarmed,*
> *Collecting all his might, dilated stood,*
> *Like Teneriff or Atlas, unremoved:*
> *His stature reached the sky, and on his crest*
> *Sat Horror plumed; —*"

after this unforgetable and heroic figure, Milton dismisses him from the poem in the scene in hell, where, returning after his triumph to take the applause of his host, he is, in the moment of his highest boasting, transformed into the serpent with all his followers in like forms — a scene so repellent that perhaps none has been more adversely commented on. This gradual degradation of Satan, in his form, is, it seems to me, a cardinal point in the poem. It is to be associated with Milton's idea of beauty — that Platonic idea which I mentioned. The first observation of Satan in hell is the lost brightness of Beelzebub whom he addresses:

> " *If thou beest he — but oh, how fallen! how changed*
> *From him, who, in the happy realms of light*
> *Clothed with transcendant brightness, didst outshine*
> *Myriads, though bright! —* "

When he comes to the new creation, the radiance of the sun reminds him of the same change in himself, and when the young angel surprises him in Eden, it is his lost beauty that he mourns.

> " *So spake the cherub: and his grave rebuke,*
> *Severe in youthful beauty, added grace*
> *Invincible, abashed the Devil stood*
> *And felt how awful goodness is, and saw*
> *Virtue in her shape how lovely — saw, and pined*
> *His loss; but chiefly to find here observed*
> *His lustre visibly impaired.* "

The power of beauty over him is the last vestige of his lost nobility. Thus in Eden gazing on Adam and Eve, he says, —

> "*Whom my thoughts pursue*
> *With wonder, and could love: so lively shines*
> *In them divine resemblance;*"

and just before the temptation, in the presence of Eve, he felt her beauty to be such that —

> "*That space the evil One abstracted stood*
> *From his own evil, and for the time remained*
> *Stupidly good, of enmity disarmed,*
> *Of guile, of hate, of envy, of revenge.*"

It is only by a recovery of his evil nature that he gains power to go on with his deceit. Such relics of faded glory as his brow wore, such relics of the sense of beauty also remained in his spirit. The debasement of his form, culminating in the scorpion scene in hell, is — for Milton — one and the same thing with the corruption of his moral nature, and is in fact a principal means of characterization; for in each new act Satan takes a new form. There is nothing elsewhere in literature quite like this.

It is, however, the peculiar meanness of his revenge which most degrades Satan's character; in his rebellion against God, in his unavailing courage when powers felt and depicted as great are matched against omnipotence, in the mere ruin of such tremendous power, there are sublime elements; but in his triumph over mankind there is no true joining of forces for equal encounter — in fact Satan is never brought in contact with Adam directly — and though Paradise is surrounded with guards and watched over by Uriel in the sun, these are no real defences; mankind is felt to be unsheltered, the power of Adam and Eve to remain obedient is not so presented as to seem a match for the power of the devil, and Satan consequently appears to triumph over a weak and innocent foe, harmless to him, whom he sacrifices in a malignant spirit of revenge by ignoble and secret ways. In his own character, and apart from man, Satan embodies the Renaissance ideal of the freedom of the individual, of the affirmation of one's own life, of development of one's powers and qualities and opportunities — he is like a brilliant, unscrupulous, rebellious Italian prince having his own way with the world he is born into; to conceive of him as resembling an English rebel against the Crown, or at all indebted to that character, except perhaps in the point of resolute defiance, is, I think, to misconceive him altogether, although it is a common view. He was, on the contrary, the Renaissance prince seeking his free career, valuing individual talent and force above everything, the concentration of personal faculty, pride, ambition — and conscienceless in his determination to live all his life out. In his struggle with omnipotence, he secures respect for certain qualities of strength which in alliance with virtue are great qualities, and even in wickedness do not lose their impressiveness; but in his easy triumph over Eve in the Garden, and in its consequences to mankind, he becomes contemptible in his aim, his method, and his being.

Certain important differences in the Titan Myth as treated by Milton should be noticed. You observe that the Greek situation is reversed: the angels are the younger race of beings, and according to Greek ideas should have succeeded and thereby have asserted the principle of progress. The angels, however, were defeated. Of course, there is no room in the scheme of the universe, as Milton conceived it, for any progress — the being and the reign of God are already perfect, and progress is only the salvation of man, that is, a restoration of things. Restoration, not Revolution, is Milton's cardinal idea. It follows from this that hell is necessarily the end of the angels; it is a *cul-de-sac*, a blind alley — it leads nowhere — it has no future; the poem stops in that direction as if it had run against a wall. The denial of progress has brought everything to a standstill, with eternal damnation for the angels and ultimate restoration for mankind. It is here, I think, that modern sympathy parts company with this portion of the poem — that is, with the conception of hell in it. Our thoughts are so pledged to the idea of progress, to the thought of evolution as the law of all created beings, that the notion of hell as a kind of sink and prison of the universe finds no place for itself in our minds. The only thing in civilization that resembles hell is the modern jail, and that we desire most potently to eliminate, in the sense that it shall not be a place that leads nowhere, even for the most hardened. I desire, however, only to set sharply over against each other in your minds the Hebrew fixity of Milton's thought and the Greek idea of progress, as they are brought out by the mythic wars of heaven in each case; and to suggest that the failure of the poem to interest the modern mind in hell, except as a spectacle, is connected with the fundamental denial of progress in it, and its departure from the thought of development.

The second great theme which Milton incorporated into his poem is the Bower of Bliss. This is the theme by means of which love, which next to war is the great subject of poetry, enters into the epic; the hero is withdrawn from battle, and tempted to forget his career in the world, by love for a woman. The importance of the theme, and its relative proportion of interest in the epic as a whole, steadily increased — it was a convenient way of withdrawing the leading character and giving the other heroes an opportunity for display free from his rivalry, it was interesting in itself as opening up the whole field of the romance and tragedy of love, and it was the best kind of an episode to vary the story. Thus the loves of

Æneas for Dido, in the " Æneid," and of Armida for Rinaldo in " Tasso," were represented. For Milton Eden is Bower of Bliss, in this sense. It freed his hand for description of nature in her softest scenes and in the atmosphere of love. You may recall Tennyson's summary of it, in his lines on Milton —

> " *Me rather all that bowery loneliness,*
> *The brooks of Eden mazily murmuring,*
> *And bloom profuse, and cedar arches*
> *Charm, as a wanderer out in ocean*
> *Where some refulgent sunset of India,*
> *Streams o'er a rich ambrosial ocean-isle,*
> *And crimson-hued the stately palm-woods*
> *Whisper in odorous heights of even.*"

Here Milton had the characteristic scenery of the Bower of Bliss, and he elaborated it with Renaissance richness of luxurious natural detail. The situation was also characteristic, and the power of woman to weaken the moral force of the hero through love was illustrated: the issue only was different, for whereas in the normal epic the hero breaks his bonds and goes back to his career — to the founding of Rome or the capture of Jerusalem — Adam was made the tragic victim of his fall, and with him all mankind. Adam, from every point of view, holds an unenviable position, for a hero: he never, as I have said is brought to a direct encounter with Satan, his great enemy, and in this round-about conflict in which he falls through the temptation of Eve his defeat is irreparable. It is singular to observe that in the only other English poem of epical action — in Tennyson's "Idylls of the King," Arthur is similarly a hero of defeat; the breaking of the Round Table is the catastrophe, brought about by the sin of Guinevere in the orthodox conventional way, and Arthur, when he sails away "to heal him of his grievous wound" leaves a lost cause behind him in the world. It would be a curious enquiry — could one answer it — why the two great epic poems of the English represent the cause of the higher life as suffering a temporary overthrow in this world. Not to enter upon that, however, I have only time to point out that, as it seems to me, modern sympathy also parts company with Milton in this portion of the poem, inasmuch as it has grown unnatural for us to regard womanhood as the peculiar means by which moral character is impaired, and the world lost; rather we go with Spenser in his conviction that womanhood is the inspiration of noble life. The character of Eve as Milton drew it is from a very ancient world of myth and race-thought: the influence of chivalry on the worldly side, and on the spiritual side the influence of the beatification of motherhood in the Virgin Mary, have profoundly affected and changed the ancient thought, and though not unfelt in Milton they have not sufficient power in him to modify essentially the primitive conception of Eve. It is the more unfortunate that Milton's own temper, as a husband, was such that he has vigorously emphasized in his poem the inferiority of woman to man, her natural subjection to him, and in general has left to her only that loveliness and charm which most appealed to him as a poet.

The third great theme of Milton is a cosmogony — that is, a story of creation: it is told by Raphael to Adam, and it is supplemented by the history of mankind which is shown to Adam prophetically by Michael. It has been the fashion of science to ridicule, as Huxley did, Milton's description of the origin of living creatures; but as a tale of creation, his story is quite the most consistent and nobly imaginative of any that poets have told, and his panorama of history is effectively unrolled, with comprehensiveness, vigour of thought and vividness of scene. In two respects, nevertheless, modern sympathy parts company with Milton here, too. He adopted as his scheme of the universe of space, you remember, the older or Ptolemaic idea, that the earth is the centre, and is surrounded by the spheres, one inside another, till you reach the outermost or *primum mobile.* He knew, of course, the Copernican scheme, which we now all hold, when we think of the relation of the earth to the sun and stars. It was, I think, the classical prepossession of his mind — his desire for a world limited, closed and clear, like a Greek temple — which led him to adopt this older scheme of the universe. But the result is that the rest of the poem is apt to seem as antiquated as its celestial geography. Again, in his view of history, he necessarily made human history unroll as a consequence of the fall of Adam, and gave an importance to its Biblical events, which they can only retain in a limited way. The centre and movement of history are now so differently conceived by the general modern mind that Milton's account of history has little essential interest to the reader.

Such, as it lies in my mind, is the composition of the "Paradise Lost" — a Titan Myth, a Bower of Bliss, and a Cosmogony or story of creation and history, blended into one unified poem in which the central event is the fall of Adam. It is a poem of the Renaissance, the last great product of that movement flowering in the far and Puritan North; it is enriched with all the treasures of the New Learning, softened with all the imaginative graces of humanism; and in the great character of Satan, it presents, on his noble side, the most magnificent embodiment of the Renaissance ideal of free and imperious individuality, and on his ignoble side it reflects some of the fairest gleams of Platonic philosophy. I have indicated in what important ways it seems disconnected with the modern mind, in its scientific and historic schemes, in its primitive view of the evil of womanhood, and in its opposition to the idea of progress. I should perhaps sum this last idea to a point, and say that in the poem the charter of free-will which the Creator gives to the angels and to Adam operates as a limitation on omnipotence; it is impossible for the modern mind to look on the Creator except as the giver of good; and yet his gift in this poem so operates as to make his omnipotence continually manifest in the act of damnation; it operates to damn the angels through their revolt, to damn Adam through his fall, and to damn mankind through Adam. Within the limits of the action described, the poem is thus from the first line to the last a poem of the damnation of things, in which the fact of final partial restoration is present as an intention and promise only. This is what makes it a poem of past time, and removes it far from the modern mind. For the democratic idea — which is the modern mind — is a power to save: it will have no prisons of vengeance, no servile nor outcast races, no closed gates of hopeless being. "Paradise Lost" is thus set behind us, as an embodiment of a historical phase of the Christian idea — like Dante.

I am aware that the verdict seems adverse to Milton; but it is not so in reality, though I desire to make plain the fact that "Paradise Lost" is now a historical poem, a past event in the imaginative life of the race. But no words I can use would sufficiently express the admiration which this poem excites in me — not merely for its unrivalled music, nor for its style which Matthew Arnold thought keeps it alive, but for its construction as an act of intellect, for its sublime imagination in dealing with infinite space, infinite time, and eternity and the beings of eternity; for its beautiful surface in the scenes in Paradise, its idyllic sweetness and charm, the habitual eloquence and noble demeanour in the characters; nor do I find its later books less excellent, in which austere thought and nakedness of idea more appear — the characteristics of the poet coming into his own, and content with truth unadorned, simple and plain — the sign and proof, of which "Paradise Regained" and "Samson Agonistes" are greater examples, that as a poet he was perfected. Small in amount, indeed, is the verse that I have read more often; such strength, such exquisiteness, such elevation, he has no rival in, for power and grace, for refinement; his voice is master of his theme; and he is seated in the heavens of poetry where Shelley saw him —

"*The third among the sons of light.*"

The Torch

VII

WORDSWORTH

We approach our own times; and if, hitherto, literature has seemed to us a somewhat far-off thing, a thing of the Greek Myth, of chivalric allegory, of the Renaissance hero, it should now grow near and fast to us as our chief present aid in leading that large race-life of the mind whose end, as I have said, is to free the individual soul. The notion that poetry is a thing remote from life is a singular delusion; it is more truly to be described as the highway of our days, though we tread it, as children tread the path of innocence, without knowing it. Nothing is more constant in the life of boy or man than the outgoing of his soul into the world about him, and this outgoing, however it be achieved, is the act of poetry. It is in the realm of nature that these journeys first take place; nature is a medium by which the soul passes out into a larger existence; and as nature is very close to all men, perhaps our experience with her offers the most universal, certainly it offers the most elementary, illustration of the poetical life which all men, in some measure lead. Wordsworth is, pre-eminently, a guide in this region; and, as he was less indebted than poets usually are to the great tradition of literature in past ages, poetry in him seems more exclusively a thing of the present life, contemporary and altogether our own. Such a poet, endeavouring by a conscious reform to renew poetry in his age and bring it home to man's bosom, eliminating the conventional ways, images, and language even of the poetic past, is necessarily thrown back on nature, in the external world, and on character, in the internal world, for his subject-matter; history, except in contemporary forms, will be far from him, and of myth and chivalry, of Plato and the Italians, though he will have his share, he will have the least possible. This may leave his verse bare and monotonous in quality, but what substance it does contain will have great vitality, for it comes directly from the man. You will observe, however, that his narrower scope of learning, treatment, and theme makes no difference in the essential point of interest. His longest and most deliberate poem — that one into which he tried to empty his entire mind, as I said the other night — "The Prelude," is the history of the formation of his mind, he says; that is, plainly, his subject is the same as Spenser's — how in our days is a human soul brought to its fullness of power and grace? The manner, the story, the accessories, the entire colour and atmosphere, are changed from what they were in the Elizabethan times, but the question abides. Spenser is hardly aware that nature has anything to do with forming the soul; to Wordsworth, nature seems its chief nourishment and fosterer, almost its creator. I desire to illustrate how Wordsworth represented the outgoing of the soul in nature, as a part of its discipline, its education in life, like the quest of the Knights in Spenser.

When you go out to walk alone in a scene of natural beauty, your senses are first excited and interested; but often there arise in consequence feelings and ideas harmonious with the scene, and emotionally touched with it, which gradually absorb your consciousness; and at last you find yourself engaged in a mood — perhaps of memory — from which the external scene has entirely dropped away or round which it is felt only as a nimbus or halo of beauty, or mystery or calm. This happens constantly and normally to all of us, and it is an act of poetry; for it is the very method and secret of the lyric. The poet receiving some impulse through his senses delights in it, and rises by natural harmony to feelings and ideas that belong with such joy, and ends in the higher pleasure to which his senses have served him as the stairway of divine surprise. Such a poem is Burns's

"Highland Mary"; he begins with the outer scene, woods and the summer, and you will notice how at the end all has dropped away except the love in his heart:

"*Ye banks, and braes, and streams around*
The castle o' Montgomery,
Green be your woods, and fair your flowers,
Your waters never drumlie!
There simmer first unfald her robes,
And there the langest tarry;
For there I took my last fareweel
O' my sweet Highland Mary.

How sweetly bloomed the gay green birk,
How rich the hawthorn's blossom,
As underneath their fragrant shade,
I clasped her to my bosom!
The golden hours, on angel wings,
Flew o'er me and my dearie;
For dear to me, as light and life,
Was my sweet Highland Mary.

Wi' monie a vow, and lock'd embrace,
Our parting was fu' tender;
And, pledging aft to meet again,
We tore, oursels asunder;
But oh! fell death's untimely frost,
That nipt my flower sae early!
Now green 's the sod, and cauld 's the clay,
That wraps my Highland Mary.

Oh, pale, pale now, those rosy lips,
I aft hae kissed sae fondly;
And closed for aye the sparkling glance,
That dwelt on me sae kindly!
And mouldering now in silent dust,
That heart that lo'ed me dearly!
But still within my bosom's core
Shall live my Highland Mary."

His heart has taken the place of all the world as Mary's dwelling.

This experience, this course of emotional thought, is the habit of the human heart; it is repeated countless times in any man's life. In each case the poem depends only on where we stop our minds. We may stop in the outer scene, and have only beautiful description: we may go on into the mood of imagination or memory, and end there; we may go further, and reach some contact with divine things, with God in nature. It is easy to illustrate the matter from Wordsworth, for he has himself defined these stages. You remember his account of his boyish skating on the ice:

" *— All shod with steel*
We hissed along the polished ice, in games
Confederate, imitative of the chase
And woodland pleasures, — the resounding horn,
The pack loud-bellowing, and the hunted hare.

So through the darkness and the cold we flew,
And not a voice was idle: with the din
Meanwhile the precipices rang aloud;
The leafless trees and every icy crag
Tinkled like iron; while the distant hills
Into the tumult sent an alien sound
Of melancholy, not unnoticed, while the stars,
Eastward, were sparkling clear, and in the west
The orange sky of evening died away.

Not seldom from the uproar I retired
Into a silent bay, — or sportively
Glanced sideway, leaving the tumultuous throng,
To cut across the reflex of a star,
Image, that, flying still before me, gleamed
Upon the glassy plain: and oftentimes,
When we had given our bodies to the wind,
And all the shadowy banks on either side
Came sweeping through the darkness, spinning still
The rapid line of motion, then at once
Have I, reclining back upon my heels,
Stopped short; yet still the solitary cliffs
Wheeled by me — even as if the earth had rolled
With visible motion her diurnal round!
Behind me did they stretch in solemn train,
Feebler and feebler, and I stood and watched
Till all was tranquil as a summer sea."

Any boy, who has skated on the river, has lived that poem: has had the physical sense of the scene, which arouses in him a certain reverberation of feeling. The second stage — that of youth — is as usual, though in Wordsworth it was uncommonly prolonged and intense:

> "*Though changed, no doubt, from what I was when first*
> *I came among these hills; when like a roe*
> *I bounded o'er the mountains, by the sides*
> *Of the deep rivers, and the lonely streams,*
> *Wherever nature led: more like a man*
> *Flying from something that he dreads, than one*
> *Who sought the thing he loved. For nature then*
> *(The coarser pleasures of my boyish days,*
> *And their glad animal movements all gone by)*
> *To me was all in all. — I cannot paint*
> *What then I was. The sounding cataract*
> *Haunted me like a passion: the tall rock,*
> *The mountain, and the deep and gloomy wood,*
> *Their colours and their forms, were then to me*
> *An appetite: a feeling and a love,*
> *That had no need of a remoter charm,*
> *By thought supplied, or any interest*
> *Unborrowed from the eye. — That time is past,*
> *And all its aching joys are now no more,*
> *And all its dizzy raptures.*"

Here the physical scene is less felt — the excitement, the reverberation, is greater. There is the third stage, to which in this poem he immediately passed on:

> "*For I have learned*
> *To look on nature, not as in the hour*
> *Of thoughtless youth; but hearing oftentimes*

The still, sad music of humanity,
Nor harsh nor grating, though of ample power
To chasten and subdue. And I have felt
A presence that disturbs me with the joy
Of elevated thoughts; a sense sublime
Of something far more deeply interfused,
Whose dwelling is the light of setting suns,
And the round ocean, and the living air,
And the blue sky, and in the mind of man:
A motion and a spirit, that impels
All thinking things, all objects of all thought,
And rolls through all things."

Here the physical scene has become abstract and elemental — diaphanous beauty — and he is in the presence of the divine power shining through its veils. Nature, beginning with the awe of boyhood, ripening into the passion and high delight of youth, matures in manhood in the spiritual insight which makes the daily process of life in merely living under the sky and in sight of earthly beauty an act of worship. It is plain, as I said, that the degree to which any man may live Wordsworth's poem depends only on where his mind stops in its ordinary human process, whether with the boy on the ice, the youth on the mountains or the man with "the light of setting suns." In all these cases, you will notice, Wordsworth represents the soul as going out from him into the large material sphere.

Wordsworth, however, was acutely conscious of the reaction of nature on mankind, of its formative power over men and their lives. The idea is most familiar to us as the influence of the environment; and we think of a sea-coast people, like the Greeks, as differing from a mountaineer people, like the Swiss, because of their natural surroundings. The idea, however, is more precise than that. The field which the farmer tills slowly bends his form to itself. You remember Millet's famous painting "The Angelus." The peasant who is its centre has been physically formed by toiling in the fields where he stands; you feel as you look, that the landscape itself is summed up, and almost embodied in him, its creature, and the picture is spiritualized, and made a type of our common humanity, by the sound of the Angelus reflected in his prayerful attitude. That is the way that Wordsworth conceived of nature as forming his dalesmen and shepherds. There is this landscape quality in all his memorable characters; you think of them, you see them, in connection with the soil. Thus you recall the figure of the Reaper; you see her at her task in the field, and the song she sings:

> " *The music of my heart I bore*
> *Long after it was heard no more*" —

that song unifies the poem and spiritualizes it, precisely

as the prayer does in "The Angelus." So you see "The Leech-Gatherer:"

> "*In my mind's eye I seemed to see him pace*
> *About the weary moors continually*
> *Wandering about alone and silently;*" —

So, too, Simon Lee, the old huntsman, and Matthew at his daughter's grave, and Michael, the builder of the sheep-fold, and Ruth, and good Lord Clifford, are landscape figures.

Wordsworth carried his thought of the formative power of nature beyond this point, and to take at once the characteristic poem, he saw nature forming the soul of a woman:

> "*Three years she grew in sun and shower,*
> *Then Nature said, 'A lovelier flower*
> *On earth was never sown;*
> *This child I to myself will take;*
> *She shall be mine, and I will make*
> *A lady of my own.*
>
> *'Myself will to my darling be*
> *Both law and impulse: and with me*
> *The girl, in rock and plain,*
> *In earth and heaven, in glade and bower,*
> *Shall feel an overseeing power*
> *To kindle or restrain.*

'She shall be sportive as the fawn
That wild with glee across the lawn
Or up the mountain springs;
And hers shall be the breathing balm,
And hers the silence and the calm
Of mute insensate things.

'The floating clouds their state shall lend
To her; for her the willow bend:
Nor shall she fail to see
Even in the motions of the storm
Grace that shall mould the maiden's form
By silent sympathy.

'The stars of midnight shall be dear
To her; and she shall lean her ear
In many a secret place
Where rivulets dance their wayward round,
And beauty born of murmuring sound
Shall pass into her face.

'And vital feelings of delight
Shall rear her form to stately height,
Her virgin bosom swell;
Such thoughts to Lucy I will give
While she and I together live
Here in this happy dell.'"

The poem comes to its climax in the thought that "beauty born of murmuring sound, shall pass into her face." There is nothing extravagant in the idea. You have all seen a face transfigured while listening to music, or to the sea; and the thought is that such listening being habitual, the expression becomes habitual, and not only that but the peace and joy and inner harmony, which the expression denotes, have become habitual, that is, parts of character. Wordsworth displays his thought more at length in the "Tintern Alley" lines, in his counsel to his sister and his confessions of his own life with nature. In consequence of this general attitude of mind toward the educating power of nature, Wordsworth held his maxim, that we "can feed this mind of ours with a wise passiveness."

He had a faith as perfect as that of the Concord philosophers in the alms of the idle hour. And he did not mean merely that thoughts and impressions stream in on one, who expands his petals to the flying pollen of heaven, or that moral instances like the lesson of the Celandine will store his collector's box, but that intimacy — habitual intimacy with the highest truths of the soul — is reached in this way. He had the impression that childhood was especially susceptible to these influences and revelations; and the glorification of childhood which is a marked trait of his most deeply-felt verse, lies in this neighbourhood of its being to nature and nature's revelations. In his ode on the "Intimations of Immortality" in childhood he pours forth, in the most passionate and eloquent phrase, his clearest, most vivid and most penetrating intuitions of the power of nature in these ways, on the boy and the man.

Such are some of the moods in which Wordsworth conceived the operation of nature on man as moulding both general and individual life, the thoughts and emotions of men and women, and the soul of childhood, as if nature were the delegated hand of God to shape our lives, and carried with its touch some power to impart heavenly wisdom. Wordsworth, you observe, had a very primitive mind; in that act of gazing on setting suns he is not far from being a sun-worshipper: he still can believe that "every flower enjoys the air it breathes." He conceives of nature, as an element, in grand lines; and he thinks of the phases of human life even — of its great occupations, its affections and sorrows, almost as if they were parts of nature — even more closely united to it and with greater kindliness than Virgil represented them in the Georgics. This simple, primitive, elementary mind underlies his thought of childhood, too, and it appears, perhaps, most significantly in the fact that when through nature he touches on the boundaries of divine being, he achieves no more than a sense of the presence of God in nature — it is only a silent presence — he does not find, so far as I can see, at any time the voice of God there. This is the primitive mood of savage and pagan man.

Perhaps it may be well to consider for a moment the place of nature in modern life, apart from Wordsworth. Lucretius, who first took a scientific view of the world, as a poet, found in nature the inveterate hard foe of mankind: he it was who first saw the careless gods look down upon

> "*An ill-used race of men that cleave the soil,*
> *Sow the seed and reap the harvest with enduring toil,*
> *Storing yearly little dues of wheat, and wine, and oil,*
> *Till they perish.*"

Virgil, as I have said, felt rather the kindly co-operation of nature with man in producing the fruits of the field, and the flocks and herds of the hills, to feed and clothe us. Our view is not so much that of Lucretius, of the opposition, but rather of the indifference of nature. She knows not mercy, nor justice, nor chastity, nor any human virtue; and man in emerging from her world lives in a sphere of thought, conduct, and aspiration to which she is a stranger. Yet, that kindly co-operation that Virgil saw, still continues on the lower levels of life, and the great change is that, whereas of old and in his day the sense of dependence on nature, that is to say on the gods, was habitual and daily, now through the growth of the world, that dependence is no longer felt as at all supernatural; the harvest ripens or fails, but we have little thought of the gods therewith; and, in fact, the habitual sense of the dependence of our own bodies on the favour of heaven is a vanishing quality. It is a consequence of this that our life necessarily grows more purely spiritual, and such dependence on the divine as is recognized is a dependence of the soul itself, felt in the contemplative mind and much more in the life of the affections. Nature as an intermediary between God and man has lost in importance, through the growth and spread of the idea of the order obtaining in nature as against the idea of nature as a series of special providences in relation to our daily lives. I count this loss as a gain, inasmuch as it throws the soul back on its own higher nature and essential life. But there is another change. Of old the thought was of the earth and toil upon it; that was nature; now our thought of nature is of a force, which we subdue. It has come about through the extraordinary development of mechanical skill. Of old we taught the winds to waft our ships, and the waters to drive our mills; but now to take the significant example — we have enslaved the lightning. Nature has become in our thoughts a Caliban reduced to civility by being put in bonds. I have much sympathy with theoretic science; with the mind's view of the world — and I recognize its noble results, not only in philosophic thought, but in much impressionistic art. But I have all of a poet's impatience of applied science. I remember hearing a story years ago of a snail who got mounted on a tortoise: "My!" he said, "how the grass whistles by!" And when I hear people in trolley-cars talk of riding on the wings of the lightning I think of the snail. What is the speed of the lightning to the swiftness of the "wings of meditation and the thoughts of love" that the soul of Hamlet knew? Is Niagara essentially an electric-lighting plant? I have heard men of science — the same men who told me that Homer never did anything of half the importance of a theorem in mechanics — I have heard them sneer at the old Greek idea that man was the centre of the universe — the Christian idea that Milton had — the idea of George Herbert:

> "*Man is one world,*
> *And hath another to attend him:* — "

this idea was man's foolish egoism. But is it a larger idea to think of nature as man's Jack-at-all-trades? For me, I must say, science — applied science — degrades the conception of nature in narrowing it to the grooves of material use. Yet this is, in general, our modern idea — the prevailing idea — of nature. What poem of recent years has been more acclaimed than that in which a Scotch Presbyterian engineer found in his engine the idea of God? It is well that he should find the idea there, as it was well in the eighteenth century that the clock-maker should find his idea of God as a clock-maker, since that was the measure of his knowledge of God; but, for all that, the narrowing influence of these scientific conceptions is no less. Hence it is that we fall into the commonest error of men — the error of perspective, a wrong sense of the proportion of things. Our eyes are fixed on the material uses of nature, and he is great among us who sets her to some new task in cheapening steel or facilitating transportation. Now in Wordsworth there is nothing of this; he hardly notices, indeed, what to Virgil was so important, her co-operation in agriculture and the life of the farm. Wordsworth restores to us the spiritual use of nature; and the spiritual use that man makes of the world is the really important thing. With that primitive mind of his, he realizes at once the closeness with which we are cradled in nature, the universality of her life round about us:

> "*He laid us as we lay at birth*
> *On the cool flowery lap of earth;*
> *Smiles broke from us and we had ease.*
> *The hills were round us, and the breeze*
> *Went o'er the sunlit fields again:*
> *Our foreheads felt the wind and rain.*"

For the least conscious, for the semi-vital among men, nature is the blanket of God round about them; for the most spiritually-minded, nature is the ante-room to His presence, and our way to higher life. In poem after poem Wordsworth illustrates all modes of approach by which on the threshold of nature the soul grows conscious of itself; especially he shows how nature feeds the mind with beauty through the senses:

> "*Sensations sweet*
> *Felt in the blood and felt along the heart*
> *And passing even into the purer mind;*"

and thus is a chief minister to us in that building of our own world — physical, emotional, moral — each one of us for himself, which is the necessary task of all. It is not a machine that we have to make, to hew wood and draw water for us, and carry us from place to place at electrical speed; it is a world that we have to build for our souls to live in and grow through, a world of happy memory, of pure hope, of daily beauty, the world of our habitual selves, and Wordsworth shows what elements for such a world of the soul — for such a daily self — nature provides and what is the art of its construction.

To Wordsworth, however, no more than to other poets was nature the whole life: and even to him, if you stop to think about it, nature has no life of her own, but is only one mode of the soul's existence and self-consciousness. He came back at last, as all do, to man as the only subject that finally interests men. I said that in nature he found only the presence, but not the voice, of God. The voice of God he found in his own bosom, in conscience, in duty, as you remember in his ode to duty he begins:

> " *Stern daughter of the voice of God,*
> *O duty — if that name thou love —* "

The second great root of his poetry is character — moral character, and in defining and enforcing its ideals none of our poets is more truly English, more truly of the race to which character is always an engrossing and primary interest. In the poem, called "The Happy Warrior" he delineated both the public and private aspects of character, as conceived by the English, with a felicity of phrase and solidity of thought, and also with eloquent distinction, such as to place the poem apart by itself as unique in our literature. The better cxample, however, for my purposes, is the portrait of a woman — "She was a phantom of delight," — the companion-piece to that I have already read — in which he begins from the things of sense, and goes on, in the way I have described, to the moral, and finally to the spiritual sphere. Here the lyric method of poetry is again illustrated —

how, starting from the external world it becomes at last purely internal — which is the method, as you recognize, of all poetical life in essence. Apart from abstract character, the sphere of human life which Wordsworth most attended to was of course that humble life of the poor in which he was most interested because they were near to the soil, and, as he thought, nearer on that account to nature's hand. It is, however, a transparent error to think of dalesmen and shepherds as nearer to nature in this sense; it is one of the fallacies of civilized life; for Wordsworth himself is the shining example how much more, in both intimacy and fullness, was his life with nature than that of any other in his generation. Nature is not to be thought of as a kind of agricultural school education, a thing for children and dalesmen; but the same rule that holds of all the gift of life holds here, that the beneficence, the splendour and mystery of the gift, increases with the power of him who receives it. Wordsworth was the true and faithful poet of lowly lives, and as such he is endeared to humanity; he was the second great democratic poet, succeeding Burns, from whom he learned to be such, as he says; but he comes more directly and intimately into our own lives through his personal force — through his own experience of what nature meant to him.

In what sense, then, is Wordsworth a race-exponent?

Principally and distinctively in the fact that he sums up, illustrates, and amplifies the experience of the race in its direct relation to nature. With that primitive mind on which I have dwelt, he spanned the difference between the earliest and the latest thought of the race; to him, in certain moods, nature was animated with a life like our own, he believed it enjoyed its life as we do, and this is primeval belief; at the other end of progress he was as pantheistic as he was animistic here, and saw nature only as another form of divine being. Thus he contemplated nature almost as the savage and almost as the philosopher, and commanded the whole scope of human thought with relation thereto. He presented nature through this wide range as a discipline of the soul in its development; it is, first, a discipline in beauty, in the power to see and appreciate loveliness, and he especially values this as a means of building up a beautiful memory — perhaps the chief consolation of advancing life. So, in the lines to the " Highland Girl, he writes: "

> " *In spots like these it is we prize*
> *Our memory; feel that she hath eyes:*"

So he wrote again of that inward eye

> " *Which is the bliss of solitude*" —

and illustrates it by the vision of the daffodils; and in the same spirit counsels his sister:

> "*Thy mind*
> *Shall be a mansion for all lovely forms,*
> *Thy memory be as a dwelling place*
> *For all sweet sounds and harmonies.*"

Secondly, it is a discipline of the emotions, which nature evokes and exercises. The emotion is represented, nearly always I think, as that reverberation of feeling which I spoke of. Perhaps its most spiritualized example is in Tennyson:

> "*Tears, idle tears: I know not what they mean,*
> *Tears from the depth of some divine despair,*
> *Rise in the heart, and gather to the eyes*
> *In looking on the happy autumn fields,*
> *And thinking of the days that are no more.*"

The reverberation of emotion, here, is the poem. It is this reverberation, truly speaking, which Wordsworth interprets as the sense of the divine presence in nature:

> "*A presence that disturbs me with the joy*
> *Of elevated thoughts*" —

Thirdly, it is a discipline of the moral sense. Here, perhaps, we have most difficulty in going along with Wordsworth. When he says:

> "*One impulse from a vernal word*
> *They teach you more of man,*
> *Of moral evil and of good*
> *Than all the sages can:*"

when he writes of himself as

> "*Well pleased to recognize*
> *In nature, and the language of the sense,*
> *The anchor of my purest thoughts, the nurse,*
> *The guide, the guardian of my heart, and soul*
> *Of all my moral being*" —

we do not readily understand his meaning. Yet if you recollect his life, as his poems disclose it like a series of anecdotes of what happened to him, you see not only how often he returned from his rambles in the hills with a strengthened moral mind in consequence of some lesson he may have derived from some flower or cloud, which spelled out for him in an image of beauty his secret thought, or set up by an initial impulse that train of feeling which resulted in meditative moral thought, but how much more often he returned so strengthened by the sight of some human incident, history or character which to him wore the aspect of a fact of nature; for he did not discriminate between nature and its operation in the lives of common folk; all life is necessarily moral, and nature by passing influentially into the lives of his dalesmen and shepherds became thereby moral in essence; nature exceeded its bounds here, in the moral sphere, just as in becoming divine it exceeded its bounds in the spiritual sphere. Wordsworth was no pantheist; he had the dews of baptism upon him and remained in the pews of the establishment all his life; but, both in his pantheistic verse, and in his verse ascribing moral wisdom to nature, he sincerely described certain experiences of his own in which he derived religious emotion and moral strengthening and enlightenment through his contact with nature and the natural lives of his neighbours on the moors and the hills. Emotion was always mainly fed in him, imaginatively, from the forms of nature; and the strengthening of emotion, and the habit of it, necessarily builds up the moral nature of man — it is the mode of its nurture. I am accustomed to say that Keats is a poet to be young with, and that Wordsworth is a poet to grow old with. The element of habit counts for much in such communion with nature as Wordsworth illustrates; for it is not any flash of thought he brings, any revelation of emotional power as a sudden discovery of the soul; the power of nature has begun to steal upon the boy, in his skating or his nutting, or his whistling to the owls, and thereafter it only grows. Meditation, too, is a large element in the habit Wordsworth establishes toward nature, and memory, as we have seen, bears a part in it. It follows that, not only is his power over his readers cumulative with years, but his attitude toward nature must have the force of habit with us before it can render to us what it rendered to him. With the formation of this habit comes that consoling power which lovers of Wordsworth find in his verse, what Arnold called the healing power of nature. I do not myself see any healing power of nature in such instances as Michael, or Ruth, of the affliction of Margaret; there are wounds which nature cannot heal, and Wordsworth was sensible of this: he did not, as Arnold says he did, look on "the cloud of mortal destiny" and put it by; no English poet can. But it is true that in the life-long appeal that Wordsworth's verse makes especially to the sober and aging mind by virtue of its equable temper, its moral strength, its simple human breadth of sympathy, as well as by its supreme rendering of the spiritual uses of nature in our daily lives, its tranquillizing power is also a main source of its hold on the general heart.

Such, in its phases, is the discipline of nature for the soul as Wordsworth presents it. The poetic act, as I have said, is the going out of the soul. If we do not fare forth on any quest of the old knightly days, yet all life consists in such a faring forth, in going out of ourselves into some larger world, practically into a club or a church or a college or a political party or a nation — in literature it consists in going out into the race-mind, in any or all its forms, into the life of the race as an idealized past, or as a part of present nature or present humanity. I have illustrated, hitherto, the imaginative or spiritual forms of history, and to-night the imaginative or spiritual forms of nature, in either of which the soul may take its course in the larger life, and going out of itself find the freedom of the universe its own — in beauty, reason, liberty, righteousness, love — the ideal elements to which all paths, whether of history or nature, lead, when imagination is the guide. It remains only to illustrate the same general theory by the example of the poet who dealt most powerfully with human life as a thing of the present as Wordsworth dealt most powerfully with nature in the same way. That is the next, and final, lecture.

The Torch

VIII

SHELLEY

In lecturing the other night on Wordsworth I did not refer to his best-known verses, the half-dozen lines which have more luminousness of language, I think, than any other English words:

> " *Our birth is but a sleep and a forgetting:*
> *The soul that rises with us, our life's star,*
> *Hath had elsewhere its setting,*
> *And cometh from afar;*
> *Not in entire forgetfulness,*
> *And not in utter nakedness,*
> *But trailing clouds of glory do we come*
> *From God, who is our home.* "

"Magnificent poetry," said John Stuart Mill, "but very bad philosophy." However that may be, the lines express the idea, natural to all of us, that we are in some sense heirs of past glory. We are accustomed to think of heredity, as something founded as it were in past time under the operation of the laws of natural selection, and stored in us physically; and embryologists say that the long series of physical changes, in consequence of which man finally became in his body the lord of living creatures, is reflected with great rapidity in the human embryo, so that when the body is born it has in fact passed through the entire race-history in a physical sense. We are no sooner born, however, than we enter at once on a new period of heredity, and acquire also with great rapidity the mental and moral powers which originally arose slowly in the race through long ages of growth, and we become civilized men by thus appropriating swiftly funds of knowledge and habits of thinking, feeling and acting; this is the education which makes a man contemporary with his time, and perhaps it normally ends in the fact, for most men, that he does what is expected of him, and also feels and thinks what is expected of him. That is the conventional, well brought up, civilized man.

There is a third sphere of heredity, with which these lectures have been concerned, in which it is more a matter of choice, of temperament and vitality, whether a man will avail himself of it, and appreciate it. Men, generally speaking, are but dimly aware of their powers and capacities outside of the practical sphere; in our growing years we require aid in discovering these capacities and exercising these powers; we require, as it were, some introduction to ourselves, some encouragement to believe we really are the power of man that we are, and some training in finding out vitally what that power of man in us is. This is our use — the earliest — of literature; it interprets us to ourselves. It does this by fixing our attention on some things that we might not have noticed — on natural things of beauty, and by providing appropriate thoughts and stimulating delightful emotion in respect to these things; or it helps us by arousing feeling for the first time, perhaps, with regard to some part of life, and by giving noble expression to such new feeling or to some emotion hitherto vague and indeterminate in our bosom; and it especially aids us by giving play to our forces in an imaginary world, where both thought and feeling may have a career which would be impossible to us in our narrow world of fact. The poverty of not only the young, but of most men, in spiritual experience, is probably far greater than men of maturity and culture readily conceive; it is possible that the forms of the church even far exceed the capacity of the people to interpret them, just as Dante, or any high work of imagination would. The poets interpret what is forming in us, and offer new objects of contemplation and emotion in the imaginary world; they go but a little way before us, for they can be read and understood only by the light of our own experience; but, hand by hand, one leads us to another till we are in the presence of the greatest. I do not know whether Shakspere unlocked his heart, as Wordsworth said, with the key of the sonnet; but I know literature is the key which unlocks our own bosoms to ourselves; though, in consequence of that respect for the individual life of the soul, which is one of the mysterious marks of man's nature, no hand but our own can turn the lock in its wards. What I described the other night as the poetic act — the going forth of the soul — must be the act of the man himself; but it is through literature that the paths make out — the highways trodden by many feet.

As you go out on these great highways of the soul, in Dante, in Shakspere, in Goethe, a strange thing will happen to you: it will seem, in the variety of new ideas, in the flood of new feeling arising in you, that you are changed within, that you have found almost a new self. I remember once when I was studying the now lost art of wood-engraving, looking as I was at hundreds of woodcuts constantly, it happened that when I went out to walk, I saw woodcuts in the landscape; my eye having grown accustomed to certain line and form-arrangements of an artistic sort, naturally picked out of the general landscape such arrangements, as you make pictures in the fire; that is to say, my eye, dwelling on this feature and neglecting that, composed the landscape, made a picture of it. Now that is the constant act of life. The human soul finds the world a heterogeneous mass of impressions; and it attends to certain things, and neglects others, and composes its picture of life that way; prefers certain memories, certain desires, and so builds its own world, as I have constantly said. It applies this method of composition even to itself. You read Byron, and before you know it you see yourself in Byron's ways, you pick out and favour your Byronic traits, you find you are Byron in your self-portrait; or you read Thackeray and find yourself in "Arthur Pendennis;" or, on the broader scale, you read Greek a good deal, Greek history and art as well as literature, and you find you see the world as a Greek world — or, again, as a French world, as the case may be. The change is a great one, amounting almost to the discovery of a new world and yourself a new self in it. So, in Goethe's life, the Italian journey and the study of the antique made a new and greater Goethe of him. So the mind of Milton, originally English, was Hebraized, Hellenized and Italianized. The discovery of the new self may be often repeated, and each new self enters into and blends with the old selves, and makes your personality, or, at least, gives form to it. So the young Roman poet was Homer and Lucretius and the Alexandrians, and is Virgil; so the young Italian was Virgil, and is Dante; so the young Englishman was Theocritus, was Catallus, was Keats, and is Tennyson. What is involved, you see, is a kind of mental embryology; just as the physical man sums up rapidly the age-long change from the lowest to the highest creature-life, just as the conventional man sums up in the same way the ages from barbarism to civilization and spans them in his education, so here the soul in its highest life — that free soul that I have spoken of — sums up and spans the difference between the ordinary man and the highest culture the race has ever known, and now holds in his own spirit that accumulation, that power of man, which (by heredity entered into of his own choice) makes him an heir of past glory — for the splendour, the leading light, the birthlight of which Wordsworth's verse is none too extravagant an expression.

Literature, then, is the key to your own hearts; and going out with the poets you slowly or swiftly evolve new life after new life, and enter partially or fully on that race-inheritance which is not the less real and sure because you must reach out your hand and take it instead of having it stored in your nerves and senses at birth; predispositions to appropriate it are stored even there, but it is a thing of the spirit and must be gathered by the spirit itself. You will, perhaps, pardon one word of warning. This process that I have described is a vital process, a thing of life, and it must be real. There is always at work that selective principle by virtue of which you compose life in the ways most natural to you. It may well happen that some great author does not appeal to you, and the reason is that you have not in yourself the experience to read him by; moreover, being a process of life, this process is one of joy, and if any author, no matter how great, does not give you pleasure, the process is not taking place. Therefore, do not read books that, after a fair trial, give no pleasure; do not read books that are too old, too far in advance of you. If they are really great, they will come in time; but if, for example, Dante's "Inferno" is a weary place to your feet and your soul feels its thousand contaminations, do not stay in such a place; and so of all other books with names of awe. Honesty is nowhere more essential than in literary study; hypocrisy, there, may have terrible penalties, not merely in foolishness, but in misfortune; and to lie to oneself about oneself is the most fatal lie. The stages of life must be taken in their order; but finally you will discover the blessed fact that the world of literature is one of diminishing books — since the greater are found to contain the less, for which reason time itself sifts the relics of the past and leaves at last only a Homer for centuries of early Greece, a Dante for his entire age, a

Milton for a whole system of thought. To understand and appreciate such great writers is the goal; but the way is by making honest use of the authors that appeal to us in the most living ways. The process that I have described is the one by which all men advance and come into their own — men of genius no less than others: for I cannot too often repeat the fundamental truth that the nature and power of the soul, its habits, its laws and growth, are the same in all men; it sometimes happens that a man who goes through the process of this high spiritual life, becoming more and more deeply, variously and potently human, developing this power of man in him, has also a passion for accomplishment — and that is one of the marks of a man of genius. Shelley was such a man; and I desire to present him, as a man with a passion for accomplishment, but also as an extraordinarily good illustration of the mode in which a man, through literature, evolves the highest self of which mankind is capable, summing up in his own soul the final results and forward hopes of the race.

At the outset let me guard against a common misconception. Shelley is too often thought of as having something effeminate in his nature, This is due, in great part, to his portrait which with all its beauty, gives an impression of softness, dreaminess and languour; in it there is little characteristically masculine. It is also due, in some measure, to the preponderance of feeling over thought in his verse, of imagery over idea, and in general of atmosphere over form; his is what we may call a colour-mind. The misconception of Shelley to which I refer is most boldly stated by Matthew Arnold, who called him an "ineffectual angel beating his beautiful wings in the void." Now nothing could be said of Shelley that is more wrong than that. Shelley was a high-spirited, imaginative child; he was a resolute Eton boy — who would not fag, you remember, and being always persistent in rebellion, carried his point; he rode, and shot the covers in his younger days, and was a good pistol-shot, all his life delighting in the practice. He was a very practical man, in business affairs, after he came of age and had learned something of human nature. He was the only man who could handle Byron with tact and reason. He made a very good will. In fact, his practical instinct developed equally with his other qualities. Neither was he a moping poet. He had fits of high spirits — of gaiety; he used habitually to sing to himself going about the house. As boy and man, both, he was typically English, aristocratically gentle in all his ways and behaviour, only nervous, impulsive, strong, wilful, quick to see, quick to respond — a very determined and active person; and, in fact, manly to the full limit of English manhood. Perhaps there is always something feminine in poetic beauty — the expression that we see typically in the pictures of St. John the Beloved; but, apart from that light on his face and that grace in all his ways, Shelley was as manly a man as they ever make in England.

This being premised, then, one reason why Shelley is so good an illustration of the development of a modern soul is the fact that the record with respect to him is so complete. No human life, with the exception possibly of Lincoln's, has been so entirely exposed to our knowledge, from his earliest days: it seems as if nothing of him could ever die, no matter how slight, boyish and trivial it might be. Thus it comes about that we see his forming mind in its first crudities. He was an eager boy, alive, awake, interested, voracious, pressing against the barrier of life for his career. He began with a taste for the most extravagant, melodramatic romance — what was then known as the German tale of wonder, in which the young Sir Walter Scott had also taken much interest; it was what we should describe as a dime-novel taste, except that its characters were monks and nuns and alchemists and wandering Jews; Shelley himself wrote two romances and many short and one long poem of this sort by the time he was sixteen years old, and published them moreover. He was always impatient, quick to act, to be doing something. His imagination was first fed by this sensationalism, and it was also scientifically excited by the spectacular side of chemical experiments; and then he began to think — at first it was politics — such things as the freedom of the press, the rights of Catholics, reform; or it was morals — such things as property, marriage; or it was metaphysics — such things as Locke's sensational philosophy, and the ideas of the age. Radical ideas in all their imperfection of newness filled his mind, reform took hold of him. He went to Ireland to make speeches, and made them, distributed tracts, subscribed to funds, helped men who were prosecuted, especially editors, got himself put under observation as a dangerous character: and not yet twenty-one years old.

There was then little sign of poetic genius in him; he had always written verses, of course, but there is no line of his early writing that indicates any talent even for good verse. But his mind had dipped in life, in thought, in action, and was impregnated with all kinds of power; especially his mind had dipped in ideas — the idea of the perfectibility of mankind, of experimental method in science, of immediate social change in England in such fundamental things as wealth and marriage. He was always a person of convictions rather than opinions; he wanted to live his thoughts, and together with his great causes he carried about a full assortment of minor matters, such as vegetarianism, for example. In a word, he began as a Reformer, and he was as complete an instance of the type as ever walked even these streets of Boston. But he found language more generally useful than action in standing forth for his ideas; and great command of language having already accrued to him through the incessant hammering of his brains on these ideas, making them malleable and portable and efficient for human use, there came to him also that intenser power of language, that passion of expression which finds its element in noble cadences and vital images of poetry as naturally as a bird flies in the air. Yet the passage from the power of prose to the power of poetry in Shelley is not a very marked advance. What he discovered, in writing "Queen Mab," his first real poem, was the opportunity that poetry gives for unfolding a great deal of matter with logical clearness and eloquent effect, with immense concentration and intensity; what he discovered was the economy of poetry, the economy, that is, of art, as a mode of expression; and, in fact, when he had written "Queen Mab" he found — to use the words I have habitually employed — that in its few hundred lines he had emptied his mind; he had done what genius always does. The poem, however, was a Reformer's poem; it contained a striking rendering of the image of the starry universe, an account of the history of man's progress, and some delicate poetical machinery in the mere setting of the piece. Its true subject was social reform. Five years later he emptied his mind a second time in the poem called "The Revolt of Islam"; in the interval he had withdrawn more from individual enterprise and special causes in the contemporary world, and had come to realize the power of literature, as greater than any he he could exercise otherwise, in the bringing of a better world on earth; but he still held to political and social reform, and wrote, under the example and in the stanza of Spenser, this allegorical tale of the Revolution and the successful reaction against it then displayed in Europe; the poem remains an inferior poem, in consequence of its material and method; but it contained all that was in Shelley's mind at the time, and was written in the model and method of what was then to him the highest art. Five years again went by, and he again emptied his mind in the "Prometheus Unbound."

In the interval great changes had taken place in him. He was still further removed from practical measures of reform — not that he ever lost interest in them — but practical reform requires a machinery that he could not provide; and he now more fully recognized the power of ideas, of eloquence to stir men's hearts, of poetry to embody images of the ideal with mastering force; and especially he recognized the fact that practical reform is a thing that from moment to moment results from abstract principles which have an eternal being. Moreover, he had fallen in with Greek, in this interval, with Greek choral poetry on the one hand, and with Greek Platonic philosophy on the other. His mind was Hellenized; like a dark cloud, his soul approached the dark clouds of Æschylus and Plato; and the contact was an electrical discharge of power: the flash of that discharge was the "Prometheus Unbound." Furthermore, Shelley's poetical faculty had developed marvellous brilliancy, sensitiveness, colour, atmosphere, sublimity of form, suffusion of beauty, and, all this, with a lyrical volume, intensity and penetration of tone, which his earlier verse had not shown. He had become, under the play of life upon him, a poet, so throbbing with the high life of the soul that he seemed like an imprisoned spirit, with the voice of the spirit, calling to men like deep unto deep; and the world seemed to lie before him transfigured, wearing a garment of outward beauty like a new morning, and, in the human breast clothed with freedom, nobility, hope, such as belongs to the forms of millennial days. Shelley had gathered into his heart the power of man that I have been speaking of, and stands forth as its transcendent example in his age. He had dropped from him, like hour-glass sand, the specific things of earlier days, things of the free press, of Catholic rights, of putting reform to the vote, of national association, of Welsh embankments — all things of detail; and also all lesser principles of property or marriage laws; he had reached the fountains of all these in the single principle of the love of man for man, which alone he was now interested to preach and spread. He had let go, too, of all revolutionary violence, as anything more than a secondary means of reform, and he clung to the principle of patience, of forgiveness, of non-resistance, as the appointed means of triumph, as I have already illustrated in the treating of "Prometheus". "I have," he wrote, in his preface, "a passion for reforming the world": it was his fundamental energy of life; but reform for him was not now to be discriminated from the preaching of Christ's Gospel. The boy who had begun with a dime-novel taste had come into such etherialized powers of imagination that the poem of "Epipsychidion" is, perhaps, the extreme instance of ideal purity in English; the boy who had begun with Locke's sensationalism had come to be the most Platonic man of his age in his spirituality: the boy who had begun with an indignant challenge to orthodoxy had come to be the voice of Christianity itself in its highest forms of moral command; the boy, who began as the practical reformer had to come to be the poet, smiting the source of all refrom in the spirit itself, and using all his powers of thought, imagination, learning, and all the means of art, to set forth the ideals of the spirit in their eternal forms. He had passed through politics, philosophy, religion — through English and French and Greek ideas — through Italian and Spanish imaginative art, and he now summed in himself that power of man which he had lived through in others — it had become his, it had become himself. In the whole course of this development no trait is more important to observe, than his marvellous intellectual honesty; he took only what at any moment was capable of living in him; he gave it free course in his life, outlived it, transmigrated from it, and came to the next stage of higher life, and so won on to the end.

The development of Shelley was as rapid as it was complete; he was not yet thirty years old when he had become the centre of human power that he was, a centre so mighty that it would be two generations before its influence in the world, and its comparative brilliancy among English poets, could begin to be measured. His genius, we now see, was that of a double personality; he had, so to speak, two selves. First, and primary in him was his social self, his public self, that by which he was a part of mankind, was interested in man, felt for man, suffered in man's general wretchedness in Europe, brooded over his destiny, formulated principles for his regeneration, and lived in the hopes, the faith, the struggle of mankind. The greater works of his mind, which he elaborated with most conscious aim to serve the world, were the ones I have named, "Queen Mab," "The Revolt of Islam" and "Prometheus Unbound," with the later, almost episodical choric drama, called "Hellas," whose subject was the Greek Revolution then going on: all these were the expression of his social self. In early life, so absorbed was he in politics, morals, and philosophy, that he hardly realized he had any life except in these; but, as years came on him with their load, he developed a personal self, private and individual, the Shelley who was alone in the world, on whom fell the burden of discouragement, the penalty of error, the blows of fortune and circumstance, the wounds of the heart; and it was in this self that his poetic power was first put forth; his sensitiveness, his response to nature, his lyrical enthusiasm, his aspiration, his melancholy; and he carried over these powers to the expression of his social self, as he carried over all his faculties and resources to that cause. But the home of his poetic genius was in his personal self; and the poems by which he is known as an artist, as a mere human spirit without reference to any special application of its life-work, are those in which the personal self is directly and spontaneously expressed, the "Alastor" being the first, and after it the "Adonais" and the "Epipsychidion"; and in addition to these longer pieces, the short lyrics, odes and stanzas, and the fragments, all of which are effusions, overflowings of his own heart. If the sense of his greatness is most supported by the larger creative works of his imagination, he is most endeared to men by these little poems of love and sorrow, of affection, of joy in nature, and of human regret. The most poignant of them are those in which the aspiration is itself a lament — and in them is the intimacy of the poet's heart. It is impossible to close one's eyes to the fact that Shelley, wholly unappreciated as he was by the public, or in private either for that matter, was deeply dejected in his last years; the personal, the artistic self, was always a relatively increasing part of his life, and he occasionally attempted great works, like the "Cenci" or "Charles II," which had no social significance. Had he lived, it can hardly be doubted he would have become more purely an artist, a creative poet, conceiving the cause of mankind more and more largely as a spiritual rather than an institutional cause, a cause of the re-birth of the soul itself rather than of the re-birth of nations. In his personal self one principle reigned supreme — the idea of love; love guided all his actions, and was the impulse of his being — love in all its forms, personal, friendly, humane; by that selective principle that I spoke of he saw life as a form of love. It is here that the true contact occurs between his personal and his social self, for he made love — the love of man for man — the principle of society regenerated as he pictured it in the "Prometheus." And again, he made love, in the "Adonais" the principle of Divine being — that Power,

> " *Which wields the world with never-wearied love,*
> *Sustains it from beneath and kindles it above.*"

Wordsworth found the presence of God

> " *In the light of setting suns,*
> *And the round ocean and the living air*" —

primarily as something external; Shelley found it primarily as something known most intimately and clearly in his own heart.

A poet of really high rank is seldom a very simple being; he is made up of many elements, some one of which usually has the power of genius, and when that is at work in him, he is great. In Shelley there are at least three such elements; he was a poet of nature, and especially he had the power to vivify nature almost as the Greek did, to give it new mythological being, as in "The Cloud." He was also a poet of man — the thought of man was like a flame in his bosom. And he was a poet of his own heart, putting his own private life into song. A poet is greatest when he can bring all his powers to bear in one act — then he gives all of himself at once. Shelley most nearly did this, I think, in the " Ode to the West Wind. " The poem arises out of nature, in the triple aspect of earth, air and ocean, held in artistic unity by the west wind blowing through them; and it becomes at its climax a poem of the hopes of mankind, and of Shelley himself as the centre of them, like a priest. So he invokes the West Wind to which by his act he has given an imaginative being as if it were the spirit of the whole visible world of air, earth and sea:

> " *Be thou, spirit fierce,*
> *My spirit, — Be thou me, impetuous one!*
> *Drive my dead thoughts over the universe*
> *Like withered leaves to quicken a new birth!*
> *And, by the incantation of this verse,*
> *Scatter, as from an unextinguished hearth,*
> *Ashes and sparks, — my words among mankind.*"

" My words among mankind. " That is not the voice of an ineffectual angel. It is the rallying cry of a great and gallant soul on the field of our conflict. When you read the " Ode to the West Wind," see in it the great elements of nature grandly presented and the cause of mankind in its large passion, and the spirit of Shelley like the creative plastic stress itself that

> " *Sweeps through the dull dense world, compelling there*
> *All new successions to the form they wear.*"

Such are some of the ways in which Shelley entered into the life of men as Wordsworth entered into the life of nature, and leads the way for those who have hearts to follow. Dip in life, as he did, with honesty, with enthusiasm, with faith, and whatever be the starting point at last you emerge on those craggy uplands of abstract and austere beauty and reason and righteousness and liberty and love —

"*Whereto our God himself is sun and moon;*" —

the fountain-heads whence flow all the streams of the ordered life of the vale. I have illustrated this process of life by the idea of the eye composing a picture; so the soul selects its most cherished desires and memories, and comes to be the soul of an artist, or a soldier, or an engineer, as the case may be. Let me vary the illustration, and say that our problem is, in the presence of the world before us lying dull and crude and meaningless at first, to charge certain things in it with our own thought and feeling, and so to give them meaning; thus our familiar rooms of the house, and the fields round about it, for example, gain a power and meaning which is for us only; the stranger does not feel the welcome that the trees of the dooryard give to him who was born under them. But we find, as our minds go out into life, things already charged with emotion and thought, like the flag or the cross; and when the flag is brought to our lips and the cross to our breast, we feel the stored emotion of the nation's life, the stored emotion of Christian sorrow, in the very touch of the symbol; life — the life of the world pours into us with power. And we find, again, ideas that are similarly already clothed with might — charged with the hearts of whole nations that have prayed for them, with precious lives that have died for them:

"*Names are there, nature's sacred watchwords*" —

liberty, truth, justice; and, if we possess our souls of them, the power of man flows into us as if we held electric handles in our palms; beaded on the poet's verse, dropt from the lips of some rapt orator, they thrill us— and the instancy, the fervour, the inspired power that then wakes along our nerves is, we feel, the most authentic sign that we are immortal spirits. And men there are, who seem like nuclei and central ganglions of these ideas, whose personality is so charged with their power that we idolize and almost worship them — what we call hero-worship. Such a man Shelley was, and is, to me. I remember as it were yesterday, when I was a freshman at Harvard, the very hour in that cold library when my hand first closed round the precious volume; and to this day the fragrant beauty of that blossomed

May is as the birth of a new life; and when I read Wordsworth's ode, —

> " *Not in entire forgetfulness*
> *And not in utter nakedness,*
> *But trailing clouds of glory do we come*" —

I think of these first days with Shelley. To others it is some other book, some other man — Carlyle, Emerson, Goethe — whoever it may be: for the selective principle always operates to bring a man to his own; but in whatever way it comes about, the seeking mind gets connected with these men, books, ideas, symbols, through which it receives the stored race-force of mankind; so each of us, passing through the forms of developing life, receives the revelation of the world and of himself, grasps the world and is able to express himself through it, to utter his nature, not in language, but in being, in idea and emotion, and becomes more and more completely man, working toward that consummation, which I began by placing before you, of the time when the best that has anywhere been in the world shall be the portion of every man born into it.

I must crave your patience for yet a final thought, which, though it may be hard to realize, yet, if it be realized only at moments, sheds light upon our days. Of all the webs of illusion in which our mortality is enmeshed, time is the greatest illusion. This race-store, our inheritance, of which I have been speaking, which vitalized in our lives is race-power, is not a dead thing, a thing of the past; all that it has of life with us is living. Plato is not a thing of the past, twenty centuries ago; but a mood, a spirit, an approach to supreme beauty, by the pathway of human love; Spenser's "Red Cross Knight" is not an Elizabethan legend, but the image of the Christian life to-day; and the hopes of man were not burnt away in the fire that consumed Shelley's mortal remains by the bright Mediterranean waves, nor do they sleep with his ashes by the Roman wall; they live in us. I have made much of the idea that all history is at last absorbed in imagination, and takes the form of the ideal in literature; it is a present ideal. We dip in life, as Shelley did, and we put on in our own personality these forms of which I have been speaking all along — forms of liberty, forms of beauty, forms of reason — of righteousness, of kindliness, of love, of courtesy, of charity, of joy in nature, of approach to God — and these forms being present with us, eternity is with us; they have been shaped in past ages by the chosen among men — by poets, by saints, by dreamers — by Plato, by Virgil, and Dante, by Shakspere and Goethe, who live through them in us; except in so far as they so live in us, they are dust and ashes: Babylon is not more a grave. But these ideal forms of thought and emotion, charged with the life of the human spirit through ages, are here and now, a part of present life, of our lives, as our lives take on these forms; casting their shadows on time, they raise us, as by the hands of angels, up the paths of being — we are released from the temporal, we lay hold on eternity, and entering on our inheritance as heirs of man's past glory, we begin to lead that life of the free soul among the things of the spirit, which is the climax of man's race-life and the culmination of the soul's long progress through time.

THE END